To: Clayton Sin

This is simply one Marine's philosophy of leading, living an ethical life and winning.

God Bless & Semper Fidelis,

Jim Brown

"Just as you would not take a hike in the woods without a map and compass, or pilot a long distance flight without GPS, you should not continue your leadership development without Dr. Jim Benson's field manual on the lessons learned from over four decades of USMC combat and private sector leadership experience. His field manual for leadership shares the wisdom only possible through experience and real-world accomplishment. I've had the pleasure of seeing Jim's lessons in action and milestones achieved through the very attributes articulated in his field manual. If you are serious about self-improvement and making a difference in the organization you lead, keep a copy of "Executive Courage; Sometimes You Have to Walk Point" in your briefcase!"

~**Anthony M. Herdener**,
Retired Chief Financial Officer, Northeast Georgia Health System
($1.3 billion/8,000 employee leading Health System in NE Georgia)

"Brilliant and practical leadership lessons from a seasoned combat veteran, coach, teacher, and mentor. Jim Benson and his leadership style are what I want my children to serve under and learn from. In a world that emphasizes self interests and gratification... this is a must read for anyone who seeks to lead with courage and change. It exemplifies the values and character that must be present in our next generation."

~**Major General Mastin M. Robeson**,
USMC (Ret) President/CEO, TRG Solutions, LLC

"Dr. Jim Benson represents the ultimate triple threat... combat-tested Marine, academic scholar, and quintessential leader. His unmatched passion, wisdom, and personal courage while president transformed two struggling military schools into two of the nation's premier leadership academies. His personal example positively impacted the lives of thousands of young men and women and ultimately assured the future of two of the nation's finest military schools. Through Executive Courage, Jim shares the wisdom gained through a life of "walking point." Jim Benson is more than merely a student of leadership; he is leadership personified."

~**Col Raymond J. Rottman**,
USAF (Ret) Executive Director, the Association of
Military Colleges and Schools of the United States (AMCSUS)

"Jim Benson, has accomplished much in his life. Other men and women have been successful but in the case of Jim Benson he has also led a life of significance. Every leader should read this book. In the Marine Corps we had a saying for those we most admired. It was, 'I would like to have you on my flank'. That was a reflection of total trust. If you would like the privilege of having Dr. James H. Benson, Colonel, USMC (RET.), on your flank, then you should buy and absorb the wisdom from Executive Courage."

~**James H. Amos, Jr.,**
Award Winning Author, Speaker, Hall of Fame
Chairman: Agile Pursuits Franchising, Inc., (Procter & Gamble)
Past Chairman: The International Franchise Association,
Chairman Emeritus: Mail Boxes Etc., now The UPS Store,
Author of three Bestsellers,
Decorated Vietnam Veteran,
International Franchise Association Hall of Fame,
Past Chairman, Tasti D Lite, Planet Smoothie,
Chairman SkinPhd, Chairman Eagle Alliance Investments

"Great book from a proven bona fide leader of young men who put his heart and soul in it."

~**Taylor D. Wilkins, Jr.,**
Managing Partner, Wilkins, Bankester, Biles, & Wynn, P.A.,
Former Chairman, Board of Trustees,
Marion Military Institute, Marion, Alabama

"I have read both of Dr. Benson's books on leadership and management while observing his amazing turnaround of my then struggling alma mater. Today, I frequently visit the wisdom from both manuals as we have turned our company into a multi-million dollar success story. In recent years, Jim has consulted with me on efficiencies, strategies, and executive hiring. He most recently accepted the chairmanship of my Board of Directors."

~**Ernest T. Lopez III,**
President, Atlanta Paving and Concrete Construction, Inc.

"I had the pleasure of serving on the Board of Directors at Riverside Military Academy. For a number of years I chaired the finance committee. During my tenure, Dr. Jim Benson was the president of the academy. He brought a unique set of skills; not only was he an educator with a military background, but he also brought strong financial skills. Jim knew how to build a budget and deliver results at year's end. He managed the staff and facilities through an extremely difficult restructuring period. He strategically reduced spending across the board and turned an annual loss of $5MM to a profit of $1-3MM per year. Jim increased our enrollment and revenue to levels not observed in many years. It was truly a pleasure to have the opportunity to work with Dr. Benson."

~**Ira J. Middleberg,**
Partner, Middleberg-Riddle Group

"For three years I served as chairman of the Board of Trustees at Riverside Military Academy while Dr. Benson served as our president. I experienced first-hand the opportunity to watch Jim dramatically increase our student population, cuts costs without harming the mission of the academy, and significantly improve the caliber of the staff and the teaching faculty, while simultaneously maintaining a high moral integrity within our community. Jim is able to get to the heart of the matter, is not afraid to make the hard choices looking you in the eye, and has an innate ability to lead others when others do not want to be lead."

~**Ken L. McKelvey,**
CPA (emeritus), RRP, Defender Resorts, Inc.

"The Board of Trustees of St. John's Military School retained Dr. Benson to assist us in evaluating the school's operation and in identifying candidates to serve as president. Jim's experience and background were quite evident as we discussed and he offered marketing strategies, financial counsel, and administration/leadership candidates for the school. Jim is committed to the education and development of young men and women, driven to complete the task at hand, follows through in a *timely manner, and is quite creative in identifying solutions to complex problems. I continue to call on Jim as he is a valuable resource to me and for our school."*

~D. Dale Browning,
Former Chairman of the Board for Frontier Airlines;
President and CEO of Colorado National Bank;
President and CEO of Plus Systems ATM; and Senior Consultant to
the Board of Visa International

EXECUTIVE COURAGE

DR. JAMES H. BENSON,
COLONEL, USMC (RET.)

EXECUTIVE COURAGE

SOMETIMES YOU HAVE TO WALK POINT

Dr. James H. Benson,
COLONEL, USMC (Ret.)

NEXT CENTURY
PUBLISHING

EXECUTIVE COURAGE
Sometimes You Have To Walk Point

Published by Next Century Publishing
Austin, TX
www.NextCenturyPublishing.com

ISBN: 978-1-68102-965-8
Library of Congress Control Number: 2017915444

Printed in the United States of America

DEDICATION

This work is dedicated to the officers and men of India Company, 3rd Battalion, 1st Marines who lived, suffered, and fought the North Vietnam regulars and Viet Cong in the rice paddies, mountains, and hamlets of South Viet Nam in 1969 and 1970.

A special mention and dedication to Paul Dukes and Mickey Hooks, snipers, attached to 2nd Platoon who were killed during August 1969. Bob Depp is another of our courageous snipers who was seriously wounded during that costly month, and is now a special friend.

Many names of those who fought courageously slip my mind these days, but I shall not soon forget Engleman, Hargett, Kazmarek, Strickland, Walker, Meadows, Upchurch, Gupton, Silvia, Price, Cole, Dewey, Hawkins, Petch, and Earl who were truly warriors and worthy of recognition, even today. God bless and Semper Fidelis.

ACKNOWLEDGEMENTS

Executive Courage is my second book, created after years of observing the human challenge, personal error, and collecting information that I thought could help leaders succeed as they shoulder the burdens of responsibility and the ever-present thorns of criticism.

There are those along the way who have made it possible for me to complete this task and its forerunner, *So You Want to be a Leader.* I must acknowledge my wife, Mary, whose love, support and tolerance were instrumental. I acknowledge my children, Catherine and Jimmy, who do not always listen to my unsolicited advice and counsel but are always loving and caring. My grandchildren, Ross and John, have unlimited potential, and I hope I have influenced their development in some small way.

There were many in the United States Marine Corps who were models of competence and integrity, and who taught me much about how to lead and administer.

I am grateful to my bosses (Board Chairmen Charles Holmes, Taylor Wilkins, Alec Fraser, Paul Gross, and Ken McKelvey) on the Boards of Trustees at Marion Military Institute and Riverside Military Academy who worked diligently with me to develop young men of character and substance.

A special thanks to Elaine Dellinger, my former secretary, long-time friend, and editor, whose insights, patience, and administrative support helped make this book possible; and Nelda Browning, my ever-competent executive secretary at Riverside Military Academy who periodically typed and retyped sections. Jo Ann Cripps was invaluable during the final months of manuscript editing. My son, Jimmy, provided edits that brought me back on track when I tended to stray from the purpose of the book. Even after all of this, Darlene Oakley from Next Century Publishing made additional improvements.

My high school coaches saw more potential in me than most of my teachers. Coach Dan Wooldridge was a terrific baseball coach and remains a lifelong friend. My college football coach, George Keim, led us to some victories we shouldn't have achieved, was a mentor with strong personal values, and remains a friend to this day. Dave Layman, Ron Ayers, Ed Knowling, Yager Marks, Bill Duke, Joe Bush, Charlie Scott, and the late John Howard Mack, high achievers in their own right and are or were loyal, lifelong friends.

I remember Phil Stone who coached me back into education and was a mentor and model of excellence, and Gordon Batchelor, my former battalion commander, friend, and editor, who writes so much better than me. John Wilbor is a loyal and longtime friend and confidant. The late coach Ray Bussard – a more loyal friend could not exist. I have learned much about entrepreneurial and bold leadership from President Ernie Lopez, friend and colleague at Atlanta Paving and Concrete Construction, Inc.

My grandmother, Hazel A. Hewitt, who gave me my core values.

To all of these and more, I am truly grateful.

PREFACE

"You can, you will, you must succeed."
Coach Raymond A. Bussard

*"...a man's accomplishments are a better window into self
than the unsound judgment and misdeeds of his youth."*
Robert Coram

In my journey from the battlefield to academia, I have become
more introspective. The things I once took for granted, I now try to
understand. Six years of doctoral study intensified my interest in the
study of human potential, especially as it related to the dimensions
of wisdom, leadership, and success. My awareness of our nation's
movement from the colonial form of wholistic education to one of
academics first and foremost is the catalyst for my philosophy of
education and development. Influenced by the writings of former
Virginia Military Institute superintendent, Josiah Bunting III, my aim
is to convince you, the reader, that success in business, government, or
academia—indeed almost any field of endeavor—requires character,
wisdom, and leadership.

The material for this book has been collected over many years and
assimilated to provide advice and counsel for those who wish to exercise
the art and science of ethical leadership. It is not for social scientists,
but for practitioners of change—those who take forlorn organizations
and make them vibrant again and those who create new organizations
destined for success. Some of the material emanates from my reading,
but most relates directly to the many leadership opportunities I have
had and the mistakes I have made as an officer in the United States
Marine Corps and as a senior administrator in middle, secondary,
and higher education but includes insights gained from reading about

mistakes others have made. Much of it appears to be common sense, but often "common sense" is detected only in retrospect. Fortunately, we can learn from others' mistakes or experiences. The focus of my message is the senior leader, male or female, who must deal with fostering change, especially in organizations that are failing. I hope my insights are practical, not theoretical.

In his book titled, *Integrity*, Dr. Henry Cloud wrote that one's personal makeup is germane to the results of the task at hand. The results, or "wake," as Cloud described it, have two parts: mission results and relationships. After a few years in an organization, one establishes a record of achievement and a record of personal dealings that make up the wake. Either dimension of the wake can be positive or negative. "The wake doesn't lie and it doesn't care about excuses," according to Cloud. Cloud's writing struck a nerve with me as I had realized, as a Marine officer, I tended to be too mission-oriented, often overlooking the fact that there is an empathetic component to leadership.

Leadership is not an end state but a process. As a senior executive, I am still learning and still making mistakes. My life has been characterized by some success, but not free from failure. Nonetheless, my mistakes today are not as egregious as those made in my earlier years. I hope the lessons I have learned and related in these pages will help increase my readers' success. I encourage my readers to consider the leadership lessons herein, but more importantly, educate yourselves through the study of leaders and their failures and successes as you cross the yard markers on the gridiron of life.

Dr. James H. Benson
Colonel of Marines (Retired)

"Virtue will have naught to do with ease;

it seeks the rough and thorny path."

Montaigne

CONTENTS

EXECUTIVE COURAGE

DR. JAMES H. BENSON,
COLONEL, USMC (RET).

INTRODUCTION

"This is the day the Lord has made;
we will rejoice and be glad in it."
Psalm 118:24

So You Want to Be a Leader—Advice and Counsel for Young Leaders
was published in 2008. Since it was updated and republished in 2012,
it has enjoyed considerable success for a self-published book. Despite
the sub-title, readers have been primarily seasoned leaders, male or
female, rather than young leaders, although it has enjoyed much success
as a text at military schools and summer leadership camps.

This sequel follows the same approach but is targeted at the
more mature leader occupying a senior executive position and those
who aspire to be an executive. It is written from the perspective of
a right-brained, Type A leader whose twenty-six years as a Marine
infantry officer and twenty-one years as a senior administrator in
three educational institutions have dramatically influenced his views
on executive performance.

In my youth, I was the neighborhood leader. I decided whether
we played army, cowboys and Indians, baseball, or football—not much
else was permitted. We played outdoors all weekend and after school
until ordered home for dinner. Board games and the like were not on
my agenda and my loyal followers (Donnie MacBrier and Michael
Robertson, primarily) were normally compliant. When they reneged,
I would bribe them by giving away my toys. In the summers when they
were absent, I rode my bike to Eureka Park where there was organized
play, but I only participated in the competitive activities such as baseball
(my favorite), box hockey, tetherball, and the like. If the Park Director
had a "crafts day," I would sulk.

When playing Army, there were normally only three or four of us, so we would have two against two or one against two (guess who was the loner). I visualized the scenario, briefed the players, and picked the teams. I grew frustrated and angry with the lack of stealth of my partner so I preferred to be alone. Little did I know how the same frustration and anger would exist later in the jungles, mountains, and hamlets of South Vietnam. Early on, I instinctively knew how to *move by bounds* (move, stop and listen, and move again), let my *"enemy"* see me, then move so quickly and quietly that I would show up behind them and end the game by mowing them down with toy guns. At other times, I would hide so well and lay in wait patiently for so long they would give up and go home to play something else. I was furious when I realized that they had abandoned my game and so willingly given up.

The skills and intuition of stealth, movement by bounds, patience, ability to envision the thoughts and possible actions of the enemy (my playmates) would later serve me well in Vietnam and in the lowlands, mountains, and shoreline of Nicaragua. In some ways, I was trained before I ever went to Quantico, Virginia, to become a Marine infantryman. I could still do it today.

Although baseball was my first love, football soon became king of my youth. In my sandlot days (one hundred pounds and under), I was a running back and inside linebacker initially (despite my size). My coach, Jerry Nagle (WDBJ television anchor, as I recall) knew football, and between me and the other halfback (Thumper Perdue) we were quite a tandem. The highest compliment Coach Nagle ever paid me was, "If we had five Jimmy Bensons nobody could touch us."

When I got to William Fleming High School, my coaches moved me from halfback to quarterback. Over the years, I contemplated the reason for that move; it certainly wasn't because of my 5'9" height. I continued to play quarterback through college, and two additional years in the military post-Vietnam. With a reasonably strong but erratic arm, I am sure I was moved to quarterback because of my leadership, competitive spirit, and good football sense. In those days, the quarterback actually called the plays and the audibles.

Later as a high school football and baseball coach, I sought to understand why some leaders were successful and others, comparable in skills, were not. Were there critical factors? As a Marine officer, I observed the difference between showmanship and leadership. I also learned that a military career was similar to an athletic coaching career. In the military, one practices for a different kind of competition where the stakes are higher, winning is a matter of life and death, and there is usually less recognition.

Research and experience have convinced me that while there are identifiable principles or "skill sets" involved in effective leadership, they cannot be applied uniformly regardless of the context in which the leadership is taking place. Tarun Khanna put it best: "... conditions differ enormously from place to place, in ways that aren't easy to codify—conditions not just of economic development but of institutional character, physical geography, educational norms, language, and culture." The executive tools analyzed in this book are most effective where they "fit" the circumstances of the situation; mis-used, they will be ineffective, or worse.

Executive Courage is written to highlight the necessity of ethical, absolute, and timely decision-making to achieve organizational success. I apply the metaphor of *walking point* to emphasize that excellence is not achieved by C.Y.A. leaders who seek cover through consensus-building, compromise solutions, focus groups, and duplicitous actions.

> **Excellence is not achieved by C.Y.A. leaders who seek cover through consensus-building, compromise solutions, focus groups, and duplicitous actions.**

Using repetition, the narrative herein deplores the *feel good culture* that abhors the occasional tension, confrontation, and conflict that accompany change in high achieving companies. Some gentle souls chafe at harmony-busting leaders who shuffle the deck—operating procedures, policies, and personnel—seeking to enhance performance and customer satisfaction. Perfect harmony is an indicator of averageness (sic) in organizational behavior and the foxhole of the lovers of stasis.

In combat, the soldier or Marine "walking point" is usually a junior enlisted man, preferably one experienced, familiar with the terrain and the tactics of the enemy. He makes countless decisions in a single combat patrol—decisions that dictate the entire patrol walking through the muck, rice paddies, or stream beds to avoid the deadly and ever-present booby-traps; selecting the time and place for security halts to listen and observe what is ahead, deciding which trails to avoid, and making other decisions that determine the safety and security of the patrol. The point man is the most exposed and will be the first to face contact with the enemy.

> ## Perfect harmony is an indicator of averageness (sic) in organizational behavior and the foxhole of the lovers of stasis.

Normally, the patrol leader is further back in the column or formation—generally number 2 or 3—but there frequently comes a time when the patrol leader decides to walk point, in spite of the danger, because his decision making responsibilities require first-hand knowledge of the situation up front. It is a decision that reflects not only courage but his responsibility for the mission and safety of the members of the patrol. It also shows the unit that he has "skin in the game," that he shares the risk, and he is one of them. It makes it impossible for him to blame someone else for the results that follow.

In the world of the executive leader, *walking point* implies an aggressive, decisive, courageous, and accountable leader who doesn't shy away from facing the problem head on, making the critical decisions, and accepting his accountability for the outcome.

Walking point refers to the numerous executive actions that require the courage, stamina, and will of the executive that remind me of the occasional decision to walk point in the mountains and rice paddies of Vietnam when contrary to standard operating procedures, the platoon commander must take the point due to the exigencies of the tactical situation. Walking point in the corner office carries its own risk. The risk may not be as lethal as in combat, but it is real. So much of the risk revolves around the will to make unpopular decisions, sometimes based on nothing more than intuition; the necessity to rock the boat by moving from stasis to change; and the courage to remove the marginal, yet popular performers and those who affect the chemistry of the organization.

> ***Walking point* implies an aggressive, decisive, courageous, and accountable leader who doesn't shy away from facing the problem head on, making the critical decisions, and accepting his accountability for the outcome.**

Walking point is taking charge. It may be a male or female leader, and it involves trusting one's instincts, a propensity to will or determine an outcome through words and action, a poorly developed sense of fear and risk, and an insatiable intention to be the best. I admit to competitive instincts that have caused me more stress than acclaim, but I have learned to hide my true competitiveness lest others detect my over-zealous need to win or for my organization to be the best of its kind. Competitive instincts are part and parcel to winning in the corner office, on the battlefield, or the gridiron.

SECTION 1

EXECUTIVE COURAGE

"An executive is a man who decides;
sometimes he decides right, but always he decides."
John H. Patterson

"What great cause would have been fought and
won under the banner I stand for consensus."
Margaret Thatcher

I have observed three kinds of courage—physical courage, moral courage and lastly, executive courage. Physical courage manifests itself most often in the actions of law enforcement officers, firemen, athletes, and military persons in combat and training. Physical courage involves overcoming fear and doing what needs to be done in spite of the odds favoring personal injury or death.

Moral courage is associated with personal values and resistance to temptation. Organizations led by those with strong personal values possess the courage to do the right thing even when it is highly unpopular internally and sometimes externally. The employees of moral organizations exhibit high morale and speak well of the company or organization.

**I have observed three kinds of courage—
physical courage, moral courage and lastly,
executive courage.**

There seems to be a positive correlation between successful performance of organizations and the presence of moral courage. Often the moral courage emanates from a form of spirituality, but I don't believe that is always the case. It is possible for organizations to be morally efficient, because the leadership is grounded in ethical behavior, fairness, and a genuine caring mindset.

Notwithstanding the importance of physical courage and moral courage, this book is about executive courage, which may encompass physical courage and moral courage, but was authored to address this rarely explained phenomenon of decisiveness under pressure, and the willingness to do the unthinkable as opposed to the often observed risk-averse behavior. Executive courage is an element of senior leadership that permits one to accept measured and calculated risk, make unpopular decisions, challenge the odds, ignore the naysayers, and weather and respond to the fallout when a decision fails to produce the hoped for results.

A leader's success is more often than not measured by his decisions—both good and bad. I have certainly made my share of both. But the rightful decisions that are hurtful to others and their families take their toll on the leader also—sometimes for days before as he ponders the decision, and for days after, frequently accompanied by criticism from others up and down the hierarchy of the organization. Most often these decisions relate to personnel.

> **Executive courage is an element of senior leadership that permits one to accept measured and calculated risk, and respond to the fallout when a decision fails to produce the hoped for results.**

There are times when an employee termination is in order even though an employee is popular and, frankly, there is nothing wrong with him except that *he just isn't good enough* to take the organization in the direction it needs to go. Frequently, the employee has a pleasant and involved spouse and ostensibly good values. Invariably, the nice spouse and family of the employee in question have a higher opinion of the employee than is rightly deserved. In this case, the leader must trust his instincts, make the unpopular decision, and accept the criticism that will invariably follow. Some will not understand, and the leader will be described as ruthless, uncaring, and more. The fact is that winning organizations seek and retain *exceptional people*. Average simply won't do.

In an interview for Harvard Business Review, legendary advisor to CEOs, Ram Chron, explained that his research found that the most common reason for failure in leadership was putting the wrong person in a job and then not dealing with the mismatch. My experience is similar except my tendency has been to stay with the change too long even though I realize the arrangement is not working.

Winning organizations seek and retain exceptional people. Average simply won't do.

My most recent failure in this regard was in the hiring of a known leader to steer the Department of Admissions and Financial Aid at a fine military college preparatory school. The individual in question possessed the leadership skills and qualities, but was wanting in terms of fit and experience. Enrollment management is the economic engine of an independent school or college, and I wasted six months deciding what to do when I knew what had to be done but, nonetheless, let feelings and friendship get in the way. Once the decision was made to terminate, the individual was better off, and so was the institution.

The most common reason for failure in leadership was putting the wrong person in a job and then not dealing with the mismatch.

A typical mistake executives make is following the opinions and consensus of senior staff and employees rather than leading them. Consensus rarely offers an optimized decision. Robert Lutz, former Chrysler CEO, coined the term *mediocra* to describe the offspring of democratic decision-making.

Second-rate leaders make second-rate decisions when they lack the force of personality to stand alone. According to General Colin Powell, "Being a great leader means sometimes pissing people off.

Trying to get everyone to like you is a sign of mediocrity. You'll avoid the tough decisions; you'll avoid confronting the people who need to be confronted; and you'll avoid offering differential rewards based on differential performance, because some people might get upset." These are the decisions that require executive courage, because one must choose the harder right over the easy wrong that often leads to criticism by board members and others within the workforce.

Executive courage differs from moral courage, because it requires an often unpopular decision to be made after thoughtful deliberation for the good of the organization, despite the fact that it will attract ill will. Retaining *challenged* employees will prevent the organization from reaching its potential or achieving the leader's vision. I see the dilemma presently as senior executives contemplate the rising cost of healthcare, as they must decide whether to terminate employees, reduce full-time hours to part-time equivalents, and or reduce the amount of company paid coverage. It will take exhaustive courage to assume the *point position* in this regard.

Walking point requires a toughness of soul, the ability to put one's feelings aside, and the force of personality to *sneer at one's fears*, notwithstanding the ensuing criticism and ill will you are about to experience. Just like walking point in Vietnam where I admonished the troops "to walk where you don't want to walk," my counsel to executives is "do what you don't want to do, and do not procrastinate in making it so."

Walking point requires a toughness of soul, the ability to put one's feelings aside, and the force of personality to sneer at one's fears.

SECTION 2

EXECUTIVE DECISION-MAKING AND THE BONEYARD

"The man who insists upon seeing with perfect clearness
before he decides, never decides."
Henri Frédéric Amiel

"Leadership is like the matador;
only the leader faces the bull."
Anonymous

Your company is not going to get to the top with an abundance of average employees, no matter how much you like them and their families. If you want an exceptional company, you must have exceptional people and, thus, you must be continuously upgrading every position in the company. Average sales people, average department heads, average marketeers, average engineers, average teachers/trainers, and average leadership will get you an average organization. The business boneyard is replete with average organizations.

How does one create an exceptional business? It is done through courageous and often painful decision-making. In his fine book, *The Conviction to Lead*, Reverend Albert Mohler wrote, "If you lead faithfully, you will make decisions that are unpopular, costly, and sometimes filled with risk. There are days when you will have to stand up and take the blame for a bad decision made by others and plenty of other days when those bad decisions were made by you. But even more frequently, leaders have to bear the burden of right decisions that hurt (others)."

Average sales people, average department heads, average marketeers, average engineers, average teachers/trainers, and average leadership will get you an average organization.

I have travelled some road in my days. From the time that I was a quarterback in high school and college, through my high school coaching, twenty-six years as a U.S. Marine officer and twenty-one years as a college and preparatory school senior executive, I have called the plays and the audibles. I am relentless in my attack on the status quo. It is clear to me that tension, conflict, and periods of chaos are the norm in ultra-high-achieving organizations, and that these phases are highly visible within first-rate companies. Although there are always exceptions, I submit that perfect harmony is an indicator of averageness and a home for mediocra. Change is the mother of progress, but it creates tension and conflict for the good of the organization.

Many failing organizations are led by, what Robert Lutz (*Icons and Idiots*, 2013) calls, "nominal or position leaders;" those who appreciate the status and temporary respect afforded organizational heads but lack the will or executive courage to make the controversial decisions to overcome organizational averageness. Nominal leaders are often very astute politically, carefully positioning themselves for the next promotion while doing nothing to rock the boat or sufficiently bold to create even a hint of failure.

Change is the mother of progress, but it creates tension and conflict for the good of the organization.

Nominal leaders are experts at forming focus groups, seeking consensus, and doing all manner of things to spread the blame in case an initiative fails. The members of the focus groups feel good just knowing they had input no matter that the decision was a compromise and, hence, sub-optimal with little chance of moving the organization forward.

Lest I over-generalize, organizations have vastly different characteristics. For-profit, non-profit, government agencies, schools and colleges, churches, and athletic teams vary dramatically in purpose and mission, but they all have one thing in common; they can be improved.

Some will survive in seemingly near-perfect harmony for a variety of reasons, but most experience some form of competition and must seek continuous improvement through change to persevere. It is the heart, soul, will, and spirit of the leader and his executive decisions that will determine organizational success and longevity.

It is the heart, soul, will, and spirit of the leader and his executive decisions that will determine organizational success and longevity.

SECTION 3

STRATEGIC AND LONG RANGE PLANNING

"No plan survives contact with the enemy."
Field Marshal Helmuth Carl Bernard von Moltke

Winning and success in the workplace, on the athletic field, or on the battlefield are closely correlated with effective execution of a plan of action. Likewise, the quality of execution is correlated with the simplicity of the plan. Intricate and complex are recipes for failure in organizational planning.

Intricate and complex are recipes for failure in organizational planning.

In combat, planning is central to everything that is done. Typically at division level and higher, the operations officer and his staff are planning the next two days of operations. Often, the plans division is planning the battle three days out or longer. At battalion, company, and platoon level, daily planning occurs to coordinate all unit movements including a fire support plan and a rudimentary logistics and communications plan. In the air, each flight is carefully planned and briefed. I am less familiar with Navy planning, but am sure that it is also based on the KISS (keep it simple, stupid) principle.

Strategic military plans and campaigns are implemented as conceived with as few changes as possible because of the coordination necessary and mutual support inherent in these types of plans.

However, since it is rare that planning precisely predicts the enemy's actions, strategic plans are generally modified by the end of day two of the campaign, and often serve only to get the friendly force ashore or on the ground prepared to fight. From then on, it is daily operational planning that carries the fight to the enemy.

Strategic military planning is an extremely complex animal, because it often incorporates at least four military services with their unique capabilities (admittedly the U.S. Army and U.S. Marines have some redundancies, but the differences in their organization and delivery means justify the existence of both). Each U.S. unified commander possesses a war and contingency planning staff and is responsible to the President and Secretary of Defense for the preparation of regional contingency plans that might be required. These plans are coordinated with the supporting commanders of the four services and are approved by the Joint Chiefs of Staff (JCS).

When I first arrived at the U.S. Southern Command in Panama in 1984, I was assigned as the "Nicaragua planner." I was a recent graduate of the Armed Forces Staff College in Norfolk, Virginia that purported to prepare majors and lieutenant colonels to be joint (all services) military planners. I soon learned that communist insurgencies were rampant in Latin America, and Nicaragua was probably the one that occupied most of General Paul Gorman's (Commander-in-Chief of the U.S. Southern Command then located in Panama) time and effort. Nicaraguan dictator, Danny Ortega, had befriended Fidel Castro and the leaders of several Soviet-Bloc countries, and intelligence existed that Ortega was considering an Iran-style U.S. Embassy seizure like the successful one in Tehran.

The deliberate U.S. joint planning process is so complex that it can take two to three years to complete a single contingency plan and, even then, it is not guaranteed that the JCS will approve it. To demonstrate how parochial and sometimes acrimonious the joint planning process was at the time, of SOUTHCOM's seven contingency plans, none had been approved by the JCS. However, to demonstrate the difference competent leadership at the top and a strong personality heading the J-5 Plans Directorate can make, within three years, SOUTHCOM completed the revision of the seven plans and two new plans (including two Nicaragua plans), and all nine were approved by the JCS. Of course, military service preferences created a great deal of compromise, which is never optimal, but a completed and approved plan with compromise is better than no plan. Moreover, in the case of Nicaragua planning, the U.S. possessed such over-whelming power that most any rational plan would have been successful if executed.

The J-5 Plans Directorate, where I was assigned, had the mission of updating the Embassy Emergency Action Plans in Central and South America, and I soon learned that the plan for the evacuation of Embassy officials and Americans throughout Nicaragua was grossly out of date. There was no detailed plan to secure and evacuate the Embassy or the Ambassador's residence, and no designated assembly area/pickup sites for other American citizens who were spread throughout the country. Some helicopter landing zones in the vicinity of the Embassy had been identified, but later I would learn that telephone wire hazards made them untenable for all but small UH-1 helicopters.

Colonel John Spoone, USAF, arrived soon after me, and became the Director of the J-5 Directorate. As I recall, we quickly learned that the Embassy Emergency Action plans in most of the high threat countries in the SOUTHCOM region required much work, and even the ones that were considered current were written by the Embassy Regional Security Officers (RSOs) who had little concept of the military forces allocated to the Regional Commander-in-Chief (CINC) General Gorman to support the region/embassies. As I read about the Benghazi fiasco in Libya, I was reminded of the situation General Gorman and Colonel Spoone inherited in Central and South America relative to Embassy security.

Soon after arrival, Colonel Spoone was directed to send a planner to Managua, Nicaragua, to meet with Ambassador Harry Bergold and the Embassy RSO. USSOUTHCOM was a joint unified command that was staffed with officers and non-commissioned officers from all four services. Ironically, in the J-5 Directorate, Plans Division, I was the only infantry officer assigned. I am sure that General Gorman and Colonel Spoone would have preferred to have an infantry planner of lieutenant colonel or colonel rank to meet with the Ambassador to Nicaragua. Moreover, I think General Gorman and Colonel Comee, his Director of J-3 (Joint Operations), both U.S. Army officers, would have preferred an Army planner over a Marine planner, but Major Jim Benson, USMC, was what they had.

I also learned that SOUTHCOM had already made an attempt to prepare an evacuation contingency plan for Nicaragua, and the results were negligible. However, the threat level based on recent intelligence and Ambassador Bergold's personal concerns had raised the priority of effort. My tasking was fairly generic: meet with the Ambassador, survey the Embassy and grounds (I wasn't sure what survey meant at that time) and the Ambassador's residence, and work with the RSO to update the Embassy Emergency Action Plan. I flew to Managua where, at the air terminal, my luggage was dropped on the floor, opened, and ransacked. Of course, my Marine haircut (it would be modified somewhat for later *visits*) attracted the attention of the Nicaraguan security to the extent that I received much *assistance* as I made my way to the Embassy sedan that was sent to pick me up.

At the Embassy, I was met by the RSO and without even checking into the Casa Grande (the Ambassador's previous residence where I was to stay), I was directed to a meeting with Ambassador Bergold, a Ronald Reagan appointee who was very aware of the security situation, knowledgeable of the absence of any detailed rescue or evacuation planning, and seemingly hungry for *first-hand* knowledge of the War between the Contras and Sandinistas in the Central Highlands. The Ambassador told me that the environment was hostile, but with proper preparation he would permit me unrestricted travel throughout the country to include the Central Highlands and contact with the Contras. The RSO told me that there was frustration that the CIA was not active out of the Embassy so very little human intelligence (humint) was being collected. However, the Army Military Attaché had been declared persona non-grata (PNG) and dismissed from the country by the Sandinistas a couple of months earlier; thus, there was good reason for the station chief (CIA) to stay close to the Embassy.

The first order of business was to complete a reconnaissance (I understood reconnaissance better than survey) of the Embassy floor plan and the Ambassador's residence, which was 4-5 miles away from the Embassy, to include entry/exit points, potential helicopter landing zones, driving time from the airport to the Embassy and residence at rush hour and other safe havens (there essentially were none), and more. I soon realized that a hurricane had destroyed the Embassy in the 1970s, and the present structure was not much more than a Butler-type steel building that would hardly survive an attack of any sophistication. It was also clear that humint would be extremely important, and General Gorman would have to have early warning of Sandinista intent and ready forces prepared to move and execute on very short notice from ship (Marines) or prepositioned (Army) somewhere nearby to defend or rescue the Embassy from attack. Moreover, the consequential evacuation of Americans during hostilities would require U.S. forces to arrive from multiple directions and means, and link up with non-combatant Americans at pre-planned assembly areas carefully communicated by Embassy officials. Some assembly areas could be identified by map reconnaissance and prior knowledge of Embassy officials, but others in remote areas would require ground reconnaissance. I could see that *mission creep* was occurring as far as my work was concerned.

Upon completion of the reconnaissance of the Embassy and the Ambassador's residence and realization that this was not going to be simply an update of the Embassy Emergency Evacuation Plan, I out-briefed with the Ambassador, RSO, and Air Force Attaché (the Ambassador offered the Attaché to assist and accompany me throughout the reconnaissance and during later forays to the Corinto seaport, Masachapa Beach, Central Highlands, Punta Huete, Somotilla, Estelli, and more). I could tell that the Ambassador had been in communications with General Gorman, and they had already concluded that there would be return visits, and humint collection away from Managua would be a task for subsequent visits.

I have never taken it lightly when someone shows confidence in me. When I returned to Panama and the written report of my findings arrived through diplomatic channels, and the results of my reconnaissance were delivered to General Gorman, I was called to a meeting with the General, and the Directors of J-2 (Intelligence), J-3 (Operations), and J-5 (Strategy and Plans). I already knew that my findings, observations, and recommendations relative to the Sandinista military in Managua were accurate, well-documented, and insightful. Ambassador Bergold had affirmed that much before I left Managua. If the *Almighty* gave me any skills readily transferable to my military vocation, it was a strong sense of organization; the ability to observe, document, and write coherent paragraphs; and the innate sense to visualize what needs to be done.

My recommendations to General Gorman were well received with the exception that he (or he and Ambassador Bergold) now wanted even more information to include a ground reconnaissance of the key terrain vicinity of the Honduran-Nicaraguan border, first-hand information relative to the Sandinista and Contra fighting in the Central Highlands, helicopter landing zone surveys in and around Managua, and so forth. Importantly, I was to be the SOUTHCOM planner for an operations plan that would bring major forces by ship and air to evacuate Americans from the Embassy and country-wide. The General's planning guidance required a near-term trip back to Managua to expedite completion of the Embassy Emergency Action plan for security and evacuation of the Embassy and Ambassador's residence first and foremost.

Soon thereafter, we organized a planning meeting at MacDill Air Force Base in Tampa to update and offer planning guidance for the supporting forces allocated to SOUTHCOM for operations in the southern region. Planners from the 18th Airborne Corps, I Marine Expeditionary Force, U.S. Air Force (tactical and strategic lift), and U.S. Navy (strategic shipping) were invited. I had written, and Colonel Spoone and General Gorman had approved, the planning guidance and general concept of operations for the Embassy and Ambassador's residence evacuation, and I presented it to the service planners at MacDill. I quickly observed the parochialism among the services. The first morning was nothing more than a *mating dance* wherein the Army wanted to be the sole evacuation force while the Marines, because of their ability to come from the sea on short notice without use of Nicaraguan airports, thought they were better suited to execute the entire operation. I was surprised at the naiveté of my own service (Marines) in that they could not fathom that an Army four-star General was not going to ignore the capabilities of his own service and turn the operation over to the Marines. Moreover, the 18th Airborne Corps planners were first-rate (my observations were that the Marines placed their best officers in operations and the Army placed their best in plans) and quickly concluded that they had specific humint needs to construct their supporting plan and would eventually send a planner to Nicaragua with me. Subsequently, the Marines would also send a planner to accompany me to the Masachapa Beach and crop duster airport near Corinto that would eventually cause us to get lost and temporarily look down the barrels of six Nicaraguan AK-47s.

Over the next ten months, I led reconnaissance and human intelligence collection efforts that took us into harm's way too many times to relate. One of the first missions out of Managua was to recon the Corinto seaport facility to confirm whether or not the shipping crates observed from aerial photography were MIG-style aircraft. This mission failed as we could not find a route across the inlet to the port without going through Sandinista security check points. During the planning of this mission, I was reminded by the SOUTHCOM Director, J-2 (Intelligence) that if we were apprehended our stories had to be plausible and consistent, because our actions in Nicaragua had ceased to be evacuation planning and reconnaissance, and would now be considered espionage by the Sandinistas. During the same *visit*, I led a successful reconnaissance effort to the Estelí Airfield and confirmed that the Sandinistas possessed the Soviet-made HIPP helicopter, but that the previously reported and superior HIND helicopter was not present or observed at Estelí. Soon thereafter, a night reconnaissance of the under-construction Punta Huete Airfield failed due to security concerns and our inability to get our vehicle close enough to facilitate a hasty escape and evasion, if discovered.

The beach reconnaissance mission was successful as we reconnoitered the defenses (which were minimal) and gradient of the Masachapa Beach and concluded that it was an ideal beach landing site for Marine forces with adequate roads to Managua. We accomplished this tasking under the guise of tourists and, fortunately, observed few Sandinista military or security officers.

The search for a C-130 capable airfield nearby was also accomplished, unfortunately accompanied by temporary detainment by the Sandinista patrol mentioned previously. American beer and cigarettes were the bribe of choice that got us out of this debacle, which occurred because we violated a simple rule "not to take a road if you don't know where it is going." This was not the only mistake that created a pucker factor for us.

We knew that most service stations would not sell gasoline to gringos, so we kept two 5-gallon cans carefully hidden in the back of the rented Chevrolet Blazer. This was not permitted by the Sandinistas, so we needed a concealed site to pour it into the tank.

After the failure of the mission at Corinto, we were enroute to Somotillo (vicinity of the Nicaraguan and Honduran border and key terrain) and were being tailed by a jeep with four Sandinista soldiers. For some reason, they always tailed us by getting in front of our Blazer. This was helpful because, when we turned, they would have to turn around, catch up, and get in front of us again, relieving any doubt of their intent. On this day, the Blazer was down to an eighth of a tank of gas, and we feared stopping in plain sight of the *tail*. It was important to see the defenses around Somotilla, because of the town's disposition relative to the best tactical route across the Honduran border into Nicaragua.

We knew Somotillo was a stretch from a safety point of view, but the Army planner accompanying me insisted that the mission was a priority, so I acquiesced. As the fuel situation became critical, we had two options—turn around and hope the Sandinista soldiers did not accompany us, which was unlikely, or pull off the road, refuel, and bribe the Sandinistas with beer and cigarettes. We chose the latter and, sure enough, faced the AK-47s once more. We had our act down by now, so with beer on our breath and a contrived routine, we showed our U.S. driver's licenses and leave papers (part of our guise) and distributed beer and cigarettes to the senior NCO in the Sandinista patrol. We were relieved that there was no officer in the group, because previous encounters with Sandinista officers were hostile, and it seemed that the lower ranking Sandinistas had little decision authority.

As we approached the border, it was evident that, by Sandinista standards, the defenses were in-depth and the main roads and intersections were covered by machine gun positions. No tanks were observed, but there were many places where they could be concealed. We had already gone too far and sought a store to purchase a soda hoping that the stop would cover our turnaround (the tail had left us soon after we gave them the bribe). Fortunately, with ten gallons of gas in the tank we were able to accomplish the maneuver and proceed towards an even more challenging mission.

The next mission was to drive up into the Central Highlands, link up with the owners of a known lodge and cantina, and seek first-hand humint on the condition of the CONTRA anti-Sandinista guerillas. Purportedly, the owners were pro-Contra and would share all they knew. Fuel remained an issue, but we knew of a town eighty or so miles away that, according to our Nicaraguan driver (an Embassy employee whose knowledge, support, and courage are impossible to describe), would provide the additional gas we would need.

Unfortunately, before we started up the mountain, we had a flat tire, which our driver changed without us leaving the vehicle. Nonetheless, this coupled with the delays around Somotillo forced us to drive into the Central Highlands during the hours of darkness.

As we approached what appeared to be the summit, lodge, and cantina, a Sandinista patrol blocked the road. This was more of a combat patrol than a security patrol as evidenced by their hostility, and they seemingly did not buy our *act*. In exchange for all of our remaining cigarettes and beer, we were finally permitted to continue on to the lodge.

Each time we were stopped, the patrols opened the back of the Blazer and looked in but did not ransack the contents, which I found strange but gratifying. There were questions to answer relative to the two empty 5-gallon gas cans. The truth that we had the extra gasoline because most service stations would not sell fuel to gringos seemed to satisfy the patrol leader's questions on that subject. Moreover, the soldiers never searched our person, although they surrounded us, covering our every move with a variety of weapons. On this dark and deserted mountain road, they could have shot us, and no one would ever have known. Not only could they have taken the beer and cigarettes, but they could have robbed us as well. Our driver and the accompanying attaché spoke fluent Spanish, and, although I had studied Spanish for four years in high school and college, I could barely comprehend the heated dialogue. When the patrol leader motioned for us to get back in the Blazer, at first I did not realize that he was permitting us to proceed to the lodge without escort.

Upon our arrival at the lodge, we checked in and were given a separate cabin with a fireplace (the temperature was twenty to twenty-five degrees lower than the lowlands), which was welcomed. The desk clerk told us that the cantina was the only place to eat, and that it would be populated with Sandinista military that night. Later that night, we met with the owners who told us that the Contras and Sandinistas used the cantina on different nights as an agreed upon stand-down and no fighting had occurred as a result. The owners provided a great deal of first-hand information, which was spot on relative to many subjects associated with the Contras' status and the nature of the two adversaries. However, we were not going to get to meet with any Contra leaders as "it was not their night" to use the cantina (an unusual arrangement, I thought).

We had eaten some bad fish at a roadside stand earlier in the day near Corinto, and we were all sick with nausea to varying degrees. Nonetheless, we had to eat something, so we decided the best cover was to walk right into the cantina, order a meal, and wash it down with Nicaraguan Rum. Notwithstanding the red beans and rice and Rum antidote, we were viewed by the Sandinista soldiers as if we were an intoxicated former boyfriend of the bride at her wedding party.

As the Sandinistas imbibed and danced with their señoritas, the hostile looks increased, and we concluded that if we made it through the night, we would leave just before sun up before the Sandinistas awakened to the reality that three gringos (probably American) had raided their party.

We paid for our lodging that night and sought an inconspicuous way to disappear back to the cabin. With little sleep due to nausea and security concerns, we departed before first light. By early morning, the nausea had subsided mostly, but we had no beer and cigarettes for bribes and no spare tire. The condition of the roads and the dangers inherent in losing another tire with no spare convinced us to stop in the mountain town of Matagalpa and try to have the damaged tire repaired. By now the sun was up, and it was Sunday morning.

The only service station we found in Matagalpa was closed, and as we parked, weighing our options, two young boys approached from between two buildings. They volunteered to take the tire for repair and take us to get some coffee. After a short hike through back streets and dilapidated buildings, we arrived at a hut-like home and met two Contras who were more than willing to describe their challenges and hardships, not the least of which included taking care of their families with the Sandinistas aware that many heads of household in this small town were fighting as Contras. We were told that their children were no longer allowed to attend school nor pick the cotton that was overdue for harvest. While we were conversing, others (presumably Contras also) repaired the tire and provided a few additional gallons of gas, which we generously paid for.

As we departed Matagalpa and the central highlands, we had a three-way discussion with much repetition to reinforce what we had observed in the previous three days (we never made a written record of our observations until we arrived back at the Embassy in Managua). The essence of my report was that we were building too large a force in our evacuation plan and follow on operations if necessary. The Sandinista Army and security forces were undisciplined, poorly trained, and amateurish in every conceivable way. However, the fact that the Nicaraguan military and security forces were seemingly incompetent had caused us to take some liberties and risks in our reconnaissance and humint collection that we knew were less than prudent. I noted this fact in my report and vowed to use greater caution on our next mission.

I offer this background to describe the complexity of military strategic planning and the requirement for humint to facilitate the detailed planning of the subordinate forces. Often, it is not possible for planners to walk the ground that they expect to fight on, but the security environment in Nicaragua and the boldness of Ambassador Bergold, General Gorman, and, later, General John Galvin (General Galvin replaced General Gorman and approved my last incursion into Nicaragua) made it possible in this case. The four services came together, and the plan was completed and approved by the JCS in record time in view of SOUTHCOM's previous history in joint planning. Unfortunately, military strategic planning is rife with compromise, unnecessary force structure, and consensus decisions because of service parochialism and the desire to "get everyone involved." Everyone wants a key role, and it is understandable, but the size of the force and the costs grow exponentially. Even then, the plan is invariably sub-optimal.

Corporate strategic planning is another animal indeed. Similar to the military strategic plan, principal staff members, department heads, and other executives come together to create the vision, mission, guiding principles, and goals of the organization. Strategic planning often purports to be a tool for organizational change. Unfortunately, after arguing for up to four days, often over nothing more than semantics, a sub-optimal plan replete with compromise is often agreed upon, only to be relegated to the shelf, never to be seen again. Nonetheless, the exercise of corporate strategic planning has value as it creates a singleness of purpose and a knowledge of the mission and values of the organization not well understood before the advent of the process.

SECTION 4

ABOVE ALL ELSE – WISDOM

*"When wisdom enters into your heart, and knowledge
is pleasant unto your soul, discretion shall preserve you,
understanding shall keep you."*
Proverbs 2:10-11

*"Knowledge is proud that it knows so much; wisdom is
humble that it knows no more."*
William Cowper

*"Wisdom and goodness are twin-born; one heart must hold
both sisters, never seen apart."*
William D. Howells

"... the price of wisdom is beyond rubies."
Job 28:18

Does anybody know? Does anybody care about the importance of being wise; wise in our business, our family lives, our social lives, and our commitment to our spiritual lives? During my morning devotions, my favorite chapters in the Holy Bible are Proverbs and Ecclesiastes, which deliver understanding, wisdom, and inspiration on how to not only survive but to succeed at work, at home, family, and more. In these chapters, King Solomon wrote what I believe is divine, inspired counsel on the nature and importance of wisdom.

King Solomon is acknowledged as the wisest man in ancient history, but according to 1 Kings of the Holy Bible, he had 300 concubines and 700 wives. How could he possibly govern and write the 31 chapters of

Proverbs and 12 chapters of Ecclesiastes with the distractions inherent in such a household?

The term wisdom and its definition have virtually disappeared from secondary and college textbooks. In fact, Webster's definitions were so weak that I wrote my own:

> Wisdom takes one from folly to discernment; it is a higher order of learning that trumps knowledge in any esoteric discipline. It is somewhat unexplainable, but encompasses academic learnings, sound judgment and common sense, intuition, discretion in language and actions, human understanding and leadership, and a sense of priorities and timing. It is the accumulation of experiential and values-based knowledge that permits one to judge, discern, decide, and live an ethical and prosperous existence.

> J. E. Dinger, Dutch professor and Japanese prisoner of World War II, cautioned his readers not to … mistake the acquisition of mere knowledge for power. Like food, these things must be digested and assimilated to become life or power. Learning is not wisdom; knowledge is not necessarily vital energy. The student, who has made himself merely a receptacle for the teacher's thoughts and ideas, is not educated; he has not gained much. He is a reservoir, not a fountain. One retains, the other gives forth. Unless his knowledge is converted into wisdom, into faculty, it will become stagnant like still water.' "[1]

Notwithstanding a bachelor's degree, two master's degrees, a doctorate, and diplomas from the Army War College and the Armed Forces Staff College, I feel over-educated and under-learned. Even when writing, I have a limited view of my own wisdom, so I corroborate it with the thoughts and quotations from those who seem to possess this quality of qualities.

---

1   Dinger, J.E., http://www.quotes.net/authors/J.E.Dinger

I am convinced that the absence of old-fashioned wisdom and the demise of our traditional family values have contributed to an American society replete with poverty, an unpredictable economy, political mayhem, failing schools, excessive crime, and more. Our schools are so focused on the acquisition of knowledge for college admissions and the first job that they seem to have forgotten there is a *second curriculum*. The *second curriculum* is wholistic in nature and is characterized by a culture of accountability that promises many rewards. This curriculum is rarely mentioned in the mission and goals of our educational centers. Its key learning outcomes are boundless and difficult to measure. Nonetheless, they are the imperatives for the development of our future leaders. In my judgment, the following imperatives are the essence of wisdom, which, when acquired, assure success and happiness.

13 Imperatives of Wisdom

1. **Sound judgment and discernment** – acute thoughts and actions, thinking that cannot manifest itself in hours, days, and weeks immersed in social media and video games.

2. **Intuition** – a sensing of what is to come and what preparatory actions are in order. It comes from experience and is a critical component of success in business and the military.

3. **Integrity and ethical decision making** – honesty in word, deed, and purpose.

4. **Confidence and poise with humility** – not arrogance—assuredness and carriage, produced by high self-esteem.

5. **A sense of purpose** – the clear intent or knowledge of a desired end state.

6. **Moral reasoning** – standards of conduct, virtuous thinking.

7. **Self-control** – self-awareness and self-discipline. A sensing and grasp of one's own emotions, desires, strengths, and weaknesses.

8. **Human understanding and leadership** – a grasp of the intentions, motivations, and desires of mankind. Admiral Rickover, the father of our nuclear Navy, cautioned that the requisite study of a naval officer is the study of man.

9. **A sense of order and preparedness** – an inherent need for order and preparedness for the unexpected. The disorganized man is a lousy tactician and leader in war and business.

10. **Selflessness** – the placement of others before self especially when in positions of authority.

11. **A sense of timing** – the ability to pick the right conditions for specific actions. It is a judgment and intuition dimension critical in military and business strategy and tactics.

12. **A sense of responsibility and accountability** – knowing that one is answerable for the outcome of the matter at hand.

13. **A spiritual connection** – maybe the most important of all. Divine guidance and intervention comes to those who seek it.

Undoubtedly, there is a strong correlation between the all-encompassing wisdom and the practice of sound judgment in the workplace, the home, or family. Virtually all of my failures were the result of immature or unsound judgment.

Sometimes, it was not what I did but when I attempted to do it that created the failure. A sense of timing is a developed instinct that one acquires from experience and acquired judgment. The more I see of the human condition, the more I believe the business of growing up is more drawn out than most believe. If one achieves wisdom and its sidekick, sound judgment, by the age of fifty, great things can happen.

There have been many instances when my choices reflected clear and present evidence of the absence of wisdom. Of course, these judgmental failures manifested themselves in consequences that provided lessons for the future.

On a particularly hot and humid day in Quang Nam Province, South Vietnam, I was leading my platoon on a ten kilometer movement to establish a platoon-size patrol base in the vicinity of a previously destroyed village named the Bo Bans. Often, when we approached a moving fresh water stream, we filled our canteens, because we didn't know when we would come upon fresh water again. Few produced truly fresh potable water, but we usually added halazone tablets to the canteens to kill any parasites, diseases, and more existing in the water source. On this day, three children approached me, they recognized me as a platoon leader by the tarnished rank insignia, and referred to me as "honcho" and volunteered to fill our canteens with fresh cold water in a trade for candy and cigarettes.

The Bo Bans were once a series of hamlets that were the havens of Viet Cong, and even though the hooches had all been destroyed, the area was still populated with the Viet Cong as evidenced by their daytime booby traps and night movement. The smiling faces on the three boys softened my heart and mitigated my judgment. When they returned the canteens were full of cool water and appeared and smelled clean.

As we took a security halt, we ate portions of a C-ration lunch and chased it with the cool water. For some undisciplined reason, many of us did not use our halazone tablets. Within thirty minutes, one half of the platoon of thirty-five to forty Marines was deathly sick with severe nausea and diarrhea. Some of us were so sick that we were incapable of continuing our advance to the previously planned destination. There is little doubt that the water was purposely contaminated, and the Viet Cong were in their tunnels laughing hysterically as we dug multiple latrines. My lack of wisdom on that day was incomprehensible.

There was another instance where experiential knowledge and common sense deserted me. While operating out of a platoon patrol base well south of the Bo-Bans noted above, we had just suffered the tragic detonation of a powerful booby trap that was tied to bamboo poles, shoulder level, and clandestinely-placed in elephant grass beside a trail. Ironically, the point man of the patrol had discovered the trip wire and the patrol leadership and his radio operator stood by the trip wire and routed the patrol around the danger, when suddenly, for unknown reason, the booby trap detonated and took out the patrol leader and the radio operator. The booby trap was a suspected artillery round that left little in bodily remains to send home. My recollection of the week or so we spent in the perilous area known as Liberty Bridge is fuzzy, but I am sure we were anxious to give the Viet Cong a taste of their own medicine.

On this particular night, we chose an ambush site right in the middle of what appeared to be an uninhabited hamlet. The trails through the hamlet were well-worn, indicating heavy Viet Cong traffic. Unable to determine the most likely avenue of approach by the Viet Cong, I decided that our reinforced, squad-sized ambush patrol would set up on the roof tops of the thatched huts that were once family homes. Getting on the roof tops and setting up our fields of fire and sectors of observation took much too long, and we had no more than settled in when I realized that the slightest movement of anyone caused the dry thatch on the roof to snap, crackle, and pop. It was now dark, with little ambient moonlight, so even though we had the elevation afforded by the roof top, observation and visibility were virtually zero. It was too late to change positions. Notwithstanding my frustration at my recent loss and hunger for vengeance, my anxiety was pegged because of our poorly selected ambush site.

I am sure that my seasoned Marines were as wary of our position as I was and actually hoping the Viet Cong did not come. My mind was racing, thinking through our options if the Viet Cong came from the east, which was our weakest direction as that was our rear security. When ambushed, the Viet Cong would rarely return fire unless their numbers were large, but they would throw grenades in every direction to create confusion and enhance their chances for escape. If encountered, I knew they would immediately realize our positions on the rooftop and that each grenade would take out three or more Marines and set the hut on fire.

The plan was to initiate the ambush with the always dependable M-60 machine gun that covered the western entrance to the hamlet. If the Viet Cong came from the east we would initiate with a claymore mine, which was dependable but only detonated once while the M-60 kept on shooting. Because of this need for complete noise discipline, there could be no discussion of our predicament among me and my element leaders.

As luck would have it, I heard movement to the east, and it was close. As the noise became clearer, it was obvious the Viet Cong were in the hamlet; our firepower was facing west and any adjustment of our position would signal our presence and permit the Viet Cong to disperse, and come at us from any number of directions. I could only hope that the rear security did not give away our presence and no one else got nervous, shifted position, and started shooting prematurely. The Viet Cong column came right through us in significant numbers and not a Marine moved. All had the self-discipline to freeze in position and realizing our vulnerability, not initiate. Later, we discussed whether we could have initiated with grenades and fought them successfully but realized that the movement to even get our grenades and pull the pin would have given us away. Since the Viet Cong column seemingly stretched the length of the hamlet, our choice of position had doomed our chances of success and ruined our one opportunity to avenge the previous loss of our two Marines. We had better options for our ambush site; my choice on that night defied all wisdom, which included my experience, training, judgment, and intuition.

As I write and explain my occasional imprudence, there were other times when wisdom and training prevailed and my decisions put some significant hurt on the Viet Cong. It seems in retrospect that when sound judgment and common sense let me down, the character, courage, and training of my Marines bailed me out.

As an infantryman in Vietnam, the laws of survival were always against you. You could get killed or maimed by an enemy ambush, a booby-trap while on patrol, shot out of the sky in a helicopter, blown up by a box mine while in a vehicle, killed by an accidental discharge by a fellow Marine, or killed carrying out an order from one above you who was unfit to command. Moreover, asinine rules of engagement (e.g., no rounds in the chamber of your M-16 or magazines in your weapon even in some high threat areas) and unreliable weapons systems such as the early versions of the M-16, which frequently jammed, plagued us constantly and decreased the odds of survival.

The Bensonian Rule for Survival was simple, but I preached it to my troop leaders continuously. The rule: "Walk where you don't want to walk (walk in the muck, rice patties, and jungle but stay off the trails, especially the trail junctions)" and "do what you don't want to do (e.g., clean your weapons continuously, maintain your personal hygiene, always dig in for the night, take frequent security halts when on the move, etc.)."

The corollary for business is, "Do what you don't want to do even when it makes you uncomfortable (terminate workers with whom you have lost trust and confidence, counsel those whose performance is slipping, encourage those who are discouraged, and get out of your office frequently, leaving the administrivia (sic) for another day)."

Hopefully, this book provides clues for the importance of the acquisition of wisdom, which offers one a better ability to apply his experiential knowledge and sound judgment in business, government, the military, and crises management.

SECTION 5

AN ENDANGERED SPECIES

"Leadership is the single most important organizational factor separating the winners and the also-rans."
David Cottrell

"Obey your leaders and submit to their authority. They keep watch over you as men who must give an account. Obey them so that their work will be a joy, not a burden, for that would be of no advantage to you."
James 1:1

"The basis of leadership is the capacity to change the mindset, the framework of another person."
Warren Bennis

"Lead, and I will follow."
Alfred Lord Tennyson

I have always been more interested in people than in things, so I guess I have become a student of people insomuch as I want to know everything there is to make them perform near their God-given abilities. In recent years, I have come to the conclusion that real leaders are an endangered species. What has become of the outspoken, emboldened, charismatic, competitive, and decisive leader who established superior standards of excellence and performance and held his charges' feet to the fire in the achievement of those standards? Yes, this is the same guy who inspired us all to levels of performance that we could never have envisioned and secured our complete loyalty to the team or organization, which he represented.

Instead, it seems that we have developed politically correct do-gooders, who socialize their way up the ladder without challenging the status quo, offending any group, or risking failure whatsoever. Such leaders tolerate incompetence and marginal performance rather than risk the confrontation or perceived leadership failure necessary to fire the culprit. Woe be unto the leader who actually displays temper or emotion and confronts the non-performer whose actions or lack thereof are affecting the success of the organization as a whole.

According to James Stockdale, retired Vice Admiral and Congressional Medal of Honor winner awardee:

> Glib, cerebral, detached people can get by in positions of authority until the pressure is on. But when the crunch comes, people cling to those they know they can trust—those who are not detached, but involved—those who have consciences, those who can repent, those who do not dodge unpleasantness. Such people can mete out punishment and look their charges in the eye as they do it. In difficult situations, the leader with the heart, not the bleeding heart, not the soft heart, but the Old Testament heart, the hard heart, comes into his own.[2]

Leaders such as those described by Vice Admiral Stockdale are not prima donnas; albeit they may be arrogant, moody, non-conforming dissenters who demand excellence and possess a low tolerance for mediocrity or idleness. They often have an extraordinary eye for detail and insist on loyalty and commitment from their employees. Likewise, they are genuinely caring and seek ways to better the lot of their people. They can motivate with a disdaining look or comment. There is never a doubt as to what is expected. They do not fear controversy; in fact,

---

2   Dr. James H. Benson, Col USMC (Ret.) *So You Want to Be a Leader: Advice and Counsel to Young Leaders.* 2nd Edition (Bloomington, IN: Trafford Publishing, 2012), 9.

they sometimes seem to relish it. Although respected, they are rarely loved by the team or work force.

According to former Indiana University and Texas Tech University basketball coach, Bobby Knight, "Popular people don't make particularly good leaders; decisive people with judgment who aren't afraid to tell other people who don't have such good judgment that their judgment isn't very good, make good leaders."

Effective leadership is the cornerstone of every corporation, military unit, Little League baseball team, small town police force, fast food restaurant, and small business. I like to call on my experience and interest in athletic success. Hence, I am continually amazed at the naiveté of the owners of professional football, basketball, and baseball teams. Seldom does the acquisition of one player turn a losing team into a winning team. Yet owners continually invest huge sums in the purchase and contract of one superstar and then skimp on the acquisition of a coach or manager whose leadership affects the performance of every player, thus changing the entire image and profit-making ability of the team.

The prudent owner starts by hiring the best manager or head coach he can find, as evidenced by his previous performance, then surrounds him with players who have demonstrated commitment, talent, personal values, and a winning attitude. True leaders are able to get average players to perform above their perceived abilities. Hence, in following years they become trading material for players with greater talent who have not reached their potential while playing for lesser managers or coaches. Although it may seem unfair, it happens all the time, and the player usually reverts to his average performance once disassociated from the leader who inspired, coached, or cajoled him to a high standard of performance.

True leaders are able to get average players to perform above their perceived abilities.

Leaders and managers often speak of the necessity of acquiring "the horses" to elevate the performance of the organization. The horses are generally viewed as the players or specialists. Not to me; the horses are the coaches and managers. If a team or department is mediocre, it probably needs a shot in the arm. It needs someone who has the force of personality to accept reality, change the expectations, raise the standards, and demand adherence to them. On the selection of leaders, "You can put a mule in the Kentucky Derby, but you have to kick his fanny all the way around the track and even then you won't win the roses or get kissed by the pretty girl."

Winning organizations seek leaders who are risk-takers, but risk-takers with common sense who judiciously manage the risk associated with change. These leaders generate action and thrive on achievement and not necessarily their own. Their glory is seeing their people excel. These organizations seek leaders who are intelligent, but not necessarily intellectual. They seek leaders who are relentless in their quest for success. They seek leaders with charisma who can motivate and inspire. They know the difference between leadership and showmanship. Showmanship seeks popularity and affirmation; leadership moves the needle to the right and is more interested in respect than popularity.

> **Winning organizations seek leaders who are risk-takers, but risk-takers with common sense who judiciously manage the risk associated with change.**

Consider the following: *When Aeschines spoke, they said, "How well he speaks, what glorious words, what magnificent tones." But when Demosthenes spoke, they shouted, "Let us march against Philip. Now."*

Leaders such as these are characterized often by:

- A frustration at things others don't observe,
- A mere tolerance for vacations,
- A life of arduous hours,
- A full measure of impatience,
- A healthy instinct for pessimism that permits them to avoid surprises; and,

- Being hard to satisfy and feeling stressed that others do not always do things to the expected standard and with the same urgency as self.

Leaders such as these are truly an endangered species.

Showmanship seeks popularity and affirmation; leadership moves the needle to the right and is more interested in respect than popularity.

SECTION 6

SETTING THE STANDARDS

"99½ won't do—got to have 100."
Wilson Pickett

"Only the mediocre are always at their best."
Jean Giraudioux

One-time French diplomat Jules Cambon said, "We have to defend the country against mediocrity: Mediocrity of soul, mediocrity of ideas, and mediocrity of action. We must also fight against it in ourselves."

Most workers will rise to the standards to which they are held. If the standards are low, they will reach or slightly exceed them. If standards are high but reasonable, they will strive to attain them. Whether publicly stated or not, the membership of the unit or organization will quickly ascertain the leader's standards and expectations. Winners set the standards high and move the goalposts back, realizing that production of a quality product challenges the athletes, soldiers, or workers, enhances the reputation of the organization, and nurtures a winner's attitude throughout the work force. Conversely, in the home or the workplace, the behavior one tolerates, he will get, and more! The human tendency is to stretch the limits or boundaries of the organization until the bell sounds signaling enough is enough.

In the home or the workplace, the behavior one tolerates, he will get, and more!

Closely akin to standards, the leader's *expectations* are the critical ingredient to performance, quality, excellence, and achievement in whatever the unit seeks to accomplish. However, standards must be enforced to have any effect on performance. Frequent restatement is also important to reseed the memory of the unit or company workers. A leader's *tolerance* of deviation from established standards magnifies itself over time to the extent that eventually there are no standards.

> **A leader's tolerance of deviation from established standards magnifies itself over time to the extent that eventually there are no standards.**

I love the Wilson Pickett song, "99½ won't do—got to have 100." It says a lot about standards. People want to be a part of a winner. They want to be challenged. Nothing demotivates more than the failure of leadership to provide a challenge or to enforce the established standards. Most of us perform better at full stretch. The feelings of accomplishment are self-perpetuating and lead to even greater levels of performance.

Most are aware of the dangers inherent in setting standards that are not adhered to by management. Steven Brown, author of *13 Fatal Errors Managers Make and How You Can Avoid Them* states that, "Standards have the desired effect only if management practices what it preaches. We cannot say one thing and do another … announced standards not adhered to become pride destroyers rather than builders."

SECTION 7

FEAR, COURAGE, AND WINNING

*"Fear is that little dark room where negatives are
developed."*
Michael Pritchard

*"I would define true courage to be a perfect sensibility of the
measure of danger,and a mental willingness to incur it."*
W. T. Sherman

We generally think of physical courage and bravery when we discuss
courage. Many writings on courage and fear relate to combat heroes.
However, real courage manifests itself more quietly when one takes a public
position that does not conform to the masses, when taking the harder
right over the easier wrong, when refusing to laugh at others' blunders,
and when voicing one's conviction with passion when the conviction will
be counter to the desires of the boss or the group as a whole.

Successful leaders also demonstrate courage when they accept
risk and make the hard choices that desert the status quo. Giving
responsibility and authority to subordinates is also courageous because
of the increased risk of temporary failure. Nonetheless, the seasoned
leader knows that subordinate growth and job satisfaction are worth
the risk of temporary failure.

**Successful leaders also demonstrate courage
when they accept risk and make the hard
choices that desert the status quo.**

Physical courage relates to one's ability to overcome real and immediate fear. According to George S. Patton, Jr., "All men are frightened. The more intelligent they are, the more they are frightened. The courageous man is the man who forces himself, in spite of his fear, to carry on. Discipline, pride, self-respect, self-confidence, and love of glory are attributes, which will make a man courageous even when he is afraid." There is truth in General Patton's statement, but he omitted what may be the greatest incentive to overcome fear and that is the internal pressure to not let one's teammates, co-workers, and friends down.

Preparation that leads to poise and confidence overcomes fear. I know fear first hand. Twice, I was caught in an open field on the receiving end of a daylight ambush with no cover or concealment. In each case, I was a platoon commander in Quang Nam Province in Vietnam. I was initially terrorized, but as the leader, I put on my *game face* and took on the appearance of controlled rage, profanely shouting orders and directing lethal fire on the Viet Cong.

I believe I learned controlled rage on the gridiron. As a quarterback in high school, college, and later in military sponsored football, I could be quite an actor in the huddle, as I profanely admonished linemen for missing their blocks and challenged backs to get the yard needed for a first down or a touchdown. In fact, I was never hesitant to call my own number on key third downs and other short yardage situations; it was much like walking point at critical times.

In Vietnam, I required daylight patrols and night ambushes to wear camouflage paint (war paint) on uncovered skin, because I wanted the Marines to look mean. I wanted the Viet Cong to fear us. But it served another purpose. It made the men feel prepared and ready, and they were. The only problem with the camouflage paint was that the stuff didn't want to wash off after the patrol, so the troops didn't like to wear it. But on the positive side, it gave them something else to bitch about, which was a favorite pastime. God love them!

One of the most courageous men I served with in Vietnam was a Hospital Corpsman (HM3) named "Doc" Hargett. Doc was a husky former high school linebacker with a strong sense of convictions. Although he stepped up often, I will never forget a morning along the Song Cu De River. I had led a platoon-sized patrol through a hamlet inhabited by Viet Cong at dusk one evening. We dropped off a two-man sniper team with a third Marine carrying a PRC-25 radio. The intent was that the sniper team would occupy a hide site until first light the next morning.

Just before daylight the snipers would maneuver to a vantage point and *take out* any Viet Cong guerillas as they attempted to exit the hamlet at dawn. The Viet Cong would frequently sneak into the hamlet at night to see family members, lady friends, and more, and leave at or near first light the next morning to occupy their cave or underground hiding place during daylight hours.

After dropping off the snipers, I moved the platoon a few kilometers away and set up a defensive position for the night. However, before 6:00 a.m. the next morning, we received a radio call that the snipers were engaged in a fire fight. We immediately saddled up and returned to the edge of the hamlet on a less than tactical dead run. Upon arrival at the hide site, we found the radio operator, Private Dewey, who said the firing had ceased about the time of his initial radio call. He feared that the snipers were dead or captured.

The two snipers, Corporal Paul Dukes and Lance Corporal Mickey Hooks, had occupied a vantage point on a small rise less than a football field's distance from the hide site. It was clear to me that someone had to go up and find the snipers. I wanted the remainder of the platoon to move to a position perpendicular to the route of movement relative to the snipers' assumed position. As I explained the plan and looked into the eyes of the squad leaders for volunteers, all began to look at their boots except HM3 Hargett who said, "I'll go." It was one of those times that I knew I had to lead, so I told the platoon sergeant to move the remainder of the platoon to a designated position and to set up a base of fire to cover our movement.

Doc Hargett and I would crawl through the elephant grass (5' to 6' high) and up the knoll in search of the snipers. It was the only time that I would ever *crawl point*. After arranging for the proper visual signals, Doc and I began our crawl forward. The sun was up by now and the climate steamy. We reached the knoll without enemy contact and found the snipers dead—they had been shot in the head, neck, and upper body multiple times. Doc immediately picked up the bigger of the two snipers, and I took the smaller one. Nonetheless, he was dead weight and was so shot up that his cranial bones rattled and his blood ran down under my shirt and flak jacket. This, coupled with the heat, caused me to become light-headed, and halfway down the hill I fell with the body shifting forward and forcing my face into the muck. I felt as if I was going to pass out and had little strength. It was as if something had cut off the adrenalin.

Somehow, while still carrying the other body, Doc helped me to my feet while adjusting my load. We gathered ourselves for a moment, then he said, "Come on, sir, let's get the hell out of here." We proceeded back to the platoon without further incident. I have never forgotten that incident. I have no idea where Doc got the strength to get me up and going while still carrying his load, which was greater than mine. I know from that point on I was barely functioning physically, and although I was the lieutenant and Doc was a hospital corpsman, he was the leader, and I was the follower for those remaining minutes.

Winning takes on a whole different dimension when it means life or death. In combat, fear is a daily companion that forces leaders to be more selfless, plan better, and think more clearly. It also elevates the senses, particularly sound and smell. The following describes a typical night time movement to and occupation of an ambush site in Vietnam.

From dusk until around 2200 (10:00 p.m.), mosquitoes were seemingly out in squadron-size with gnats flying escort. The mosquitoes' mission was to harass, infuriate, and break down the discipline of Marines as we moved by stealth to establish an ambush position to destroy the Viet Cong or NVA regulars daring to move under the cover of darkness. We could not wear insect repellent, because the enemy could smell it and detect our presence. The mosquitoes were too quick to catch, and you could not smack them because of the requirement for noise discipline—even the movement of your arm (cloth against cloth) made noise that raised the ire of every Marine present. A cough in an ambush site or during a security halt enroute to the ambush site would cause near rage in my gut.

In 1969-70 in Quang Nam Province, the Viet Cong (VC) were seemingly everywhere, but finding them during the daylight hours was rare, except when they held a covered and concealed position and a ready escape route. They knew well our capability to quickly call in artillery, mortars, and close air support. But signs of their presence discovered during daylight patrols were key to knowing where to set up the ambushes at night.

We moved in bounds, cautiously walking twenty to forty meters at a time, stopping (freezing all movement is a better description) to listen for the slightest sound of enemy presence. However, as one strains to hear, the ear plays games with the mind, and one hears noises that do not exist or convert a sound into something it isn't. When at last we reached the planned ambush site, getting set up in it was another ordeal that set nerves on end.

Casualties were so high in those days that we always had replacements that ostensibly could do nothing without whispering, kicking a rock, stumbling, and/or uttering a curse word. Some people have no concept of silence; no amount of training seems to help. I believe noise discipline is instinctive; some have it, some don't. I had three American Indians in my platoon; they could move with stealth, never doze off on watch, and hear when they were seemingly asleep.

We routinely set out claymore mines to initiate our ambushes, because they did not misfire. Setting them out front of the ambush was the first order of business once the patrol was set into position. One or more Marines moving by stealth would go forward of the ambush site and emplace the claymore mines facing the planned kill zone (facing *away* from our position!). This invariably took longer than it should, which caused more anxiety for the patrol leader as it was imperative that every member of the ambush patrol knew these Marines were in our kill zone. This was particularly dangerous as the Marines never had sufficient rest and might doze off the minute they were in place, and if awakened by noise to their front, might react in a deadly way.

Finally, once the ambush was set and everyone was in place, if the VC did come, they rarely ever came in the direction of or into the planned kill zone. They invariably arrived to our flank or the rear of the ambush! The tension and stress created by the above was compounded by fear that only departed when the shooting started.

The correlation between courage and winning is significant by any statistical measure. Likewise, the management of one's fear comes with experience and training. Someone once said that getting beaten is different from losing. Even the best organizations lose on occasion. In this section, I have offered grim examples of physical courage and the anxiety and even rage that can be caused by fear.

Courage is mental and physical. One does not have to be a soldier, fighter pilot, fireman, or law enforcement officer to show courage.

It is needed in the corporate board room, in schools, churches, and certainly in our government. For the most part, the remainder of this discussion of courage will relate to executive courage.

> **The correlation between courage and winning is significant by any statistical measure.**

SECTION 8

BE OF CONVICTION

"Tolerance is the virtue of the man without convictions."
G. K. Chesterton

*"I will listen to anyone's convictions, but pray keep your
doubts to yourself."*
Johann Wolfgang von Goethe

*"A great man is one that can develop convictions in solitude
and carry them out in a crowd."*
Søren Kierkegaard

"This Lady's not for turning."
Margaret Thatcher

I am well aware of the thorns of criticism when pressing my convictions. Moreover, the discomfort they have caused my superiors in the Marines, and later, is unfortunate. There is a difference between one's opinions and one's convictions. Conviction leads to a tenacity of purpose that overcomes the most daunting of obstacles. Opinions can be spread around with little research or evidence to support them. Convictions are different; I will fight over them, and I have probably lost as many as I have won.

I encountered many declarative people in the Marines who were often wrong but never in doubt. In self-reflection, I am also declarative and often wrong, if not in principle, in timing. I would have been a better officer if I had possessed the judgment to consider the timing of the expression and insistence upon my convictions. Timing is undoubtedly an element of wisdom wherein I was shortchanged.

My convictions about truth in government have led to a disdain for politics. The late Paul Harvey once said, "In times like these, we must remember that there have always been times like these." Truly, our democracy has forever experienced deceitful and duplicitous behavior on the part of politicians. However, the strength and wealth of the parties have increased dramatically over the years, and the support of the party is an absolute if one seeks election or reelection. The outrageous appurtenances associated with public office stain any political effort to color politics as service. Celebrity, wealth, healthcare, and retirement benefits in federal elective office exceed any in the free world. Yet, there is no accountability for their many failures.

Party-first-and-foremost conservatives and liberals have but one intent and among many, it is not the betterment of America—that intent is reelection and maintenance of the aforementioned appurtenances. Every time I see a House or Senate vote right down party lines, I shudder, because I know that votes were bought and horse traded, and the interests of our country were second to the interests and pressures of the party. Even judges, many of whom are elected, are subject to party pressure. What could be more reprehensible than to hear a Republican or Democratic judge rule continuously in a partisan way, and we the subjects must refer to them as *Your Honor*!

Robert Gates, author and former Director of the Central Intelligence Agency and Secretary of Defense under President Obama and Bush II, had this to say about Congress: "Uncivil, incompetent in fulfilling basic constitutional responsibilities, micromanagerial, parochial, hypocritical, egotistical, thin-skinned, often putting self (and re-election) before country. This is my view of the majority of the U.S. Congress."

Another political reality is the effect opinion polls have on our lawmakers and party leadership. Albert Mohler wrote, "... in the larger world of politics and world history, we can see the difference between leaders of conviction and leaders who are looking for a safe place to land." Opinion polls can cause political candidates to depart from their convictions in favor of positions that favor election. Relative to poll watching, I favor the words of the great Texan, Sam Houston, who said,

"One is bound to admire the political figure who, when great principles are at stake, has the courage to defy his constituency."

Whether in government or in business, the leader must be true to his convictions. Honesty sells in virtually every business. The business of politics is the only place I know where deceitful and duplicitous behavior offer long-term rewards. Former Georgia Senator, Max Cleland wrote, "I fear that the insidious influence of money in politics and the incessant year-round campaigning required to hold your seat on the Hill are the greatest threats to our country."

Notwithstanding the late Paul Harvey's contention, I don't believe there have ever been times like these in America. I am convinced that our great Democracy has been corrupted by money, greed, extravagant appurtenances, and the absence of term limits. The word politics has become the symbol and alibi for deceit, spin, cunning, guile, and other disingenuous behavior.

Honesty sells in virtually every business.

In closing, I call on the conviction of Emperor Marcus Aurelius (C. 160 A.D.), "For a man's greatness lies not in wealth and station, nor in his intellectual capacity, which is often associated with the meanest moral character, . . . but a man's true greatness lies in the consciousness of an honest purpose in life. . . ."

The Day I Lied to the Commandant of the U.S. Marine Corps

"Talent is a gift, but character is a choice."
John Maxwell

*"There is harmony and inner peace to be found in following
a moral compass that points in the same direction,
regardless of fashion or trend."*
Ted Koppel

*"By themselves, character and integrity do not accomplish
anything. But their absence faults everything else."*
Peter Drucker

According to former U.S. Marine Corps Commandant, General Charles Krulak, as Roman society deteriorated, tension developed between the legionnaires and praetorians, who were the imperial bodyguards. As the well-connected praetorians ascended into favor, they would strike their breastplates and shout, "Hail Caesar." To emphasize their differences from the praetorians, the legionnaires would strike their armor and shout, "Integer," which means undiminished, complete, and perfect. The legionnaire was emphasizing his character in contrast to the immoral conduct of the praetorians.

The absence of integrity is observed in many forms. Stephen Carter, author of *Integrity*, wrote that, "An integrity crisis affects U.S. society." Carter found school administrators who confuse their educational mission with winning in athletics, journalists who write their stories without the facts, schools with inflated grades and low academic standards, police corruption, and more. More recently, we see school principals and superintendents looking the other way while teachers "teach to the test" or look the other way while learning statistics are manipulated by the transfer of weak students, just before standardized tests are administered. I find it unconscionable that educators responsible for children's development are cheating in order to achieve the "No Child Left Behind" standards.

Michael Josephson, president and founder of the Josephson Institute on Ethics, writes that, "We're in a state of moral malaise." He claims that U.S. citizens are not proud of themselves, their government, or their leaders ostensibly due to the demise of our societal integrity.

I remain an admirer of former Georgia governor and Senator, Zell Miller, who wrote, "Courage is what makes the difference between a statesman, who does or says what he truly believes is right before such thoughts and actions are possible, and a politician, who says what he thinks people want to hear and leads the crowd only after he observes the direction in which it is going."

A Gallup Poll of American executives discovered that 80 percent drive while under the influence, 35 percent cheat on their taxes, 75 percent use company supplies for non-company business, and 78 percent make personal, long-distance phone calls on the company telephones. On the political scene, how as a nation do we not only tolerate the present state of political mendacity but in some corners applaud and celebrate it?

Dishonesty is most likely to manifest itself in deceit. Thus, deceit is the most hideous form of dishonesty, because its intent is to deceive. Whether its form is exaggeration of the good to cover the bad, the use of guile and cunning to promote oneself above others, or the cover up of error and failure, deceit is a cardinal sin that is next to impossible to forgive.

I appreciate Denis Waitley's story of how the surgeon tested the integrity of a new nurse in *Empires of the Mind*:

> It was the surgical nurse's first day on the medical team. She was responsible for ensuring that all the instruments and materials were accounted for before the operation was completed. As the surgeon

prepared to sew up the incision, she noticed that the surgeon had removed only 11 sponges from the patient, and she was positive they had used 12. "No, I removed them all," the doctor told her. "We'll close up now."

"No," insisted the nurse, "we used 12 sponges."

"I'll take the responsibility," said the surgeon. "I'm ready to close up now."

"You can't do that, sir," said the nurse. "Think of the patient."

The surgeon lifted his foot, revealing the twelfth sponge hidden beneath his shoe. "You'll do just fine in this or any other hospital," he said with a smile.

Deceit is a cardinal sin that is next to impossible to forgive.

Retired Marine Brigadier General Tom Draude stated, "Marines don't measure what they say against the political correctness yardstick. We deal in truth, in the lack of guile, and that sometimes will be perceived as insensitive." I am familiar with the consequences of my lack of sensitivity and the expression of my convictions when I press them, notwithstanding the discomfort and chagrin sometimes felt by my superiors. Nonetheless, I have often managed to achieve against the odds even when it did not earn the affirmation of my superiors, and I am grateful for General Draude's words. If only politicians had his kind of courage. Benjamin Disraeli reminded us that "You will find as you grow older that courage is the rarest of all qualities to be found in public life." How prophetic!

In my youth, I do not recall ever hearing a school or college discussion regarding integrity. My grandmother read the Ten Commandments to me more than a few times, but other than number nine where God gives warning about "giving false testimony against thy neighbor," there is no direct commandment relating to integrity or honesty. Moreover, I do not recall ever hearing a teacher, coach, or Melrose Baptist Church Sunday School teacher discuss this all-conquering personal characteristic.

During my teen years, lying was an everyday event. I lied about where I was going, where I had been, what I had done, why I had done it, how much homework I had, whether I had done my homework, and more. The only redeeming part of my disingenuous behavior was that often my purpose was simply not to disappoint my parents or grandparents.

It was not until I heard Staff Sergeant Blanchard, my U.S. Marine Corps Officer Candidate School (OCS) drill instructor, drive the point that integrity was the most important characteristic of a leader that I realized I was not a very honest person. It was not the last time I would hear it as the importance of integrity was pressed in every leadership class whether I was at the U.S. Army Infantry Officer Advanced Course at Fort Benning, Georgia; the Armed Forces Staff College at Norfolk, Virginia; or the Army War College at Carlisle, Pennsylvania.

In my civilian education at Bridgewater College there was an Honor Code, but my recollection is that its purpose was simply to discourage academic cheating. While a graduate student at, the University of Tennessee, the Pennsylvania State University, or the George Washington University, no one ever lectured us on the importance of being truthful and honorable. Primarily, because of my fear of having to go before the dreaded Honor Council at Bridgewater, I always sat next to the window so that I could look up from my examination and not have to worry that someone would think that I was looking at another's paper. Years later, I often recommended this strategy to my cadets.

With that as background, I vividly remember the instance where I lied to the Commandant of the U.S. Marine Corps. I cannot describe the feeling in my gut when I left his office that seemingly fateful day. Marine Lieutenant Colonel (LtCol) Rich Higgins, while serving on a Middle East peacekeeping force, was snatched (kidnapped) by Hezbollah extremists in the early 1990s. As the Southwest Asia and Middle East Marine planner working at the Headquarters, U.S. Marine Corps, each morning at 5:00 a.m., I arrived at the Pentagon to acquire the latest intelligence on LtCol Higgins' purported location and the Joint Special Operations Command's (JSOC) progress (if any) to rescue him. Subsequently, I would meet with General Al Gray, Commandant of the Marine Corps, and his three-star and two-star Deputy Chiefs of Staff and brief them on what I had learned.

To begin with, it was the most awkward briefing environment imaginable but was consistent with General Gray's folksy style. He sat at the end of a coffee table and the other General Officers sat on two sofas one on each side of the coffee table. The briefer stood at the other end of the coffee table without benefit of a lectern, flipchart, map board, or the infamous Power Point slides. So, each day I stood there clumsily handling my 5x8-inch briefing note cards *and* the map of the region. First, I would brief from my note cards (map under my arm), and then after questions I'd walk between the coffee table and the other General Officers' shoes, ever careful not to step on anyone's spit- shine. I would then stand beside General Gray, placing the small map in his lap (the other General Officers could not see the map) and with my trusty collapsible pointer trace the possible routes and timeline of the intelligence communities' best estimate of the kidnapper's route, hide sites, and destination.

On this one particular unnerving day, and upon completing the map briefing and preparing to again walk the gauntlet between the coffee table and the spit-shined shoes, I lightly kicked General Gray's highly lacquered ax handle adorned with the Marine Corps emblem and four silver stars, and a placard commemorating some special event honoring General Gray. It was leaning against the window sill and made an alarming sound when it hit the floor. I quickly put it back in place, embarrassed but glad that all accoutrements were still attached and tip-toed back to my position at the other end of the coffee table to field final questions.

Upon arrival back at my position, General Gray asked if I had talked to anyone at the Embassy in Tel Aviv.

My response was, "Yes Sir, I spoke to the Attaché just before this briefing."

His next question caused a lump in my throat, because I was not sure of the answer. General Gray asked me, "Were you on a secure phone line?"

I could have said, "I don't know" or "I will check and get back to you," but instead I answered, "Yes, Sir." I stood at the position of attention during the next few minutes of bantering by the Generals, sickened that I had been disingenuous with the Commandant of the Marine Corps. When the bantering ceased and General Gray looked back at me, it was the signal for me to take my leave. I responded with my standard conclusion, "Sir, subject to additional questions, that concludes my brief."

Upon departure, I darted back to my office for a quick look at the buttons on my phone to help me recreate the call, hopefully concluding that the call was on the secure phone line as I had stated. I knew that I had initiated the call but was still not sure if it was secure or not. I quickly told my Branch Head, Colonel Jim Murphy of my awkward experience and requested to go directly to Lieutenant General Carl Mundy (Deputy Chief of Staff, PP&O), who was present at the briefing, and confess my breach of integrity. My request was granted, and General Mundy had returned from General Gray's office and his secretary let me in.

At the position of attention, I explained the entire substance of the call and that "it was likely that the call was not on a secure line, and I didn't know how I could have made such a mistake, and that I had lied to the Commandant." The General, having been present and observing me kick over the Commandant's ax handle, twice negotiate the gauntlet, and now confess to lying to the Commandant, slightly smiled and said, "Jim, I will take care of it."

The relief I felt at the time was unexplainable. I never heard another word about the incident. I worked for General Mundy two more times, and later he placed me in command of Joint Task Force-129, Counter-Terrorism, and the Special Operations Training Group (SOTG). My follow-on briefings with General Gray were uneventful, so I will never know if Lieutenant General Mundy ever mentioned my failure to General Gray.

Since my years as a U.S. Marine Officer, I have spent twenty years as a senior administrator at the college and college preparatory school level. There has not been a student or cadet under my care and development who does not have a clear understanding of the meaning and importance of integrity and can speak on the subject with some level of knowledge, competence, and confidence. Many who served in our great military would echo my feelings of the importance of integrity and wish it upon the many politicians who have never served their country in uniform.

No one can claim perfect integrity, and all of the military services have experienced moral failure within their ranks; but there is a disdain for dishonesty within the Corps that exceeds any organization in which I have ever been associated.

In his book, *Over the Top*, Zig Ziglar encouraged leaders to conduct their lives as if, "The mike is open and the camera is on (us)." Whether we are writing a report, preparing our taxes, explaining an incident where we might have a degree of culpability, or filing an insurance claim, leaders must resist the temptation to deceive. I am convinced that everyday actions and decisions at home and at work, not made from a values-based foundation, cause problems with stability within the family, workplace, and unit.

Integer!

SECTION 10

DISHONESTY AND DISLOYALTY DESERVE NO SECOND CHANCE

"This above all: to thine own self be true,
and it must follow, as the night is to the day,
Thou canst not then be false to any man."
William Shakespeare

"Suffer long for mediocre but loyal Huns. Suffer not for
competent but disloyal Huns."
Attila the Hun

"There is no right way to do the wrong thing."
Jerry Panos

"Integrity is the DNA of character."
Tommy Newberry

Of the five most significant on-the-job mistakes I have made during my service in the Marines, and subsequent years as a senior college administrator, four involve the failure to terminate subordinates at the time my instincts told me to do so.

The three most notable reasons for termination of an employee are dishonesty or mendacity, disloyalty, and apathy on the job. The first two deserve no second chance. The third I can work with—for a while. It is, nonetheless, a challenge to try to motivate an apathetic worker. Incompetence is certainly reason for dismissal, but if an incompetent employee gives 100 percent, I usually work hard at finding a place where he can contribute.

Undoubtedly, one of the toughest and most important decisions facing an executive is when to terminate a subordinate leader or manager. The positive or negative after effects will invariably ricochet throughout the organization. Harold Geneen, the late ITT Chief Executive Officer, said, "This decision is the most acute test of the leadership of an organization." The rank and file pass judgment on what the boss did and how it was done. They respect the leader who makes the tough decision but expect compassion in the method in which it is done.

In most instances, firing an employee should be a deliberate and contemplated endeavor. It should seldom be on the spur of the moment (except in isolated cases of dishonesty and disloyalty) and generally should follow well-planned and rehearsed counseling. Counseling should be face-to-face and specific in nature. Faint praise and counseling by innuendo will not suffice. The worker must be told of his shortcomings, offered a plan for improvement, and given a fair amount of time to put the new regimen into practice. Follow-up sessions are appropriate for those who make a concerted effort to improve but still are not quite achieving the goal.

> **One of the toughest and most important decisions facing an executive is when to terminate a subordinate leader or manager.**

It has been said that leaders do not suffer fools. However, I suggest that leaders can suffer fools longer than they can suffer disloyalty and dishonesty. But it is important that the leader makes it known upfront where he stands relative to these two morale and success inhibitors.

Disloyalty manifests itself in many ways. There have been times when one of my subordinate leaders was ostensibly doing his job in a satisfactory manner while more or less patronizing his subordinates and self-promoting to the extent that I concluded I was being undermined. It is a sensing I get that tells me when a subordinate is not on the same page as I am philosophically, or he wants my job. General Colin Powell described this dilemma as well as it can be described:

Now and again it turns out that a subordinate is not in harmony with me, and I have to relieve him. This is never easy. It can be especially difficult when a subordinate has done nothing specifically wrong that warrants relief. During my assignment to the 101st, I had to relieve a commander for that hard-to-pin-down reason. He'd so far had a successful career; he'd done nothing specifically wrong that would have demanded his relief; but I never sensed that I had him, that he was in my space. He performed well enough to be seen as competent, but that was not enough. He wasn't leading to my satisfaction. He executed my instructions, but only marginally and without passion and intensity .... I was dragging a weight behind me.[3]

Do not be naïve; in every profession there are sharks who will undermine you, especially if you are successful. Yes, even in our great military where integrity is considered a core competency.

I have experienced this phenomenon three times, and each time I waited too long to make the decision to separate the subordinate. I tried counseling and performance evaluation comments that were direct and clear. They never worked, and I added significant stress to my life by procrastinating in the name of fairness.

Management expert and author, Steven Brown advises,

When you have determined in your mind that the person is destined to failure, terminate him or transfer him to a position for which he is better suited. Don't keep him around to die a slow death and suffer the agony of being undermined by you. If the other party becomes equally involved in the fault-finding, one of you had better dust off the luggage, because no one building will be large enough for both of you.[4]

---

3   Colin L Powell and Tony Koltz. *It Worked for Me: In Life and Leadership*. New York: HarperLuxe, 2012.

4   W. Steven Brown. *13 Fatal Errors Managers Make and How You Can Avoid Them*. (New York: Berkley Books, 1987), 113.

In summary:

1. Fire when necessary, but fire with compassion. Trust your instincts - when it's time, it's time. Try to let the employee being dismissed save face if at all possible. But in some cases, it may be appropriate to fire quickly and with "measured malice." The leader realizes that a backlash may occur within the organization if he appears ruthless and cold in carrying out a dismissal.

2. Resist the temptation to fire on the spur of the moment without warning or counseling, except in extreme cases.

3. Realize that you are not doing it to them, but for them, because they are a bad fit for the position and should do better elsewhere, and/or they must learn that they are accountable for their performance and behavior.

4. Never suffer dishonesty or disloyalty.

SECTION 11

POWER AND AUTHORITY – THE GOOD, THE BAD, AND THE EVIL

"Power is my mistress;
I have worked too hard at her conquest to allow anyone to
take her away from me."
Napoleon Bonaparte

"Nearly all men can stand adversity, but if you want to test
a man's character, give him power."
Abraham Lincoln

"The fundamental concept in social science is power, in the
same sense in which energy is the fundamental concept in
physics."
Bertrard Russell

"Power tends to corrupt, and absolute
power corrupts absolutely."
Lord Acton

The mention of the word power connotes an uneasy feeling among many. We tend to envision power as akin to a domineering authority figure. But in reality, power is the essence of persuasion without force; it is the leader's ability to inspire others to achieve.

Of course, throughout history, power has been abused to the extent many fear it. The new leader's use of power will be closely observed and evaluated by the team, unit, or work force. The experienced leader will expect as much and will be extremely judicious in the use of recently acquired power, especially in the early days and weeks after assuming a position of authority.

Power is the essence of persuasion without force; it is the leader's ability to inspire others to achieve.

Numerous psychological studies report that the need to influence others through power is a greater need among leaders than the need to be liked or even to achieve personally. Experienced and successful leaders use power surreptitiously and in a way that preserves a harmonious balance.

Power and authority are virtually synonymous terms. But power can have a sinister connotation. Authority is more subtle. How a leader uses power is directly related to the success he is able to bring about.

Experienced and successful leaders use power surreptitiously and in a way that preserves a harmonious balance.

It is known that power has the capacity to corrupt. History is replete with individuals whose egos enlarged dramatically with the assumption of significant authority over others. Often, power is viewed as the culprit when seemingly good people become engaged in unethical activities. Some in power come to believe that they are above the company regulations and even the law. We have all observed how the assumption of a position of power can cloud the judgment of the leader. Thomas Babington summed it up well: "The highest proof of virtue is to possess boundless power without abusing it."

Power placed in the hands of the non-leader can be fraught with danger. He may resort to coercive power that uses threats and sanctions to achieve compliance and obedience. John Gardner, in his fine book, *On Leadership*, wrote,

... we must not confuse leadership with power. Leaders always have some measure of power rooted in their capacity to persuade, but many people with power are without leadership gifts. Their power derives from money, or from the capacity to inflict harm, or from control of some piece of institutional machinery ....[5]

In summary, the nature of leadership relates to how the leader uses the power associated with his organizational authority. Except in the exigencies of combat, police work, and firefighting, absolute and immediate response to direction from the leader is rarely prescribed. In other situations, a more subtle, deliberate, and persuasive use of power should be the norm.

How a leader uses power is directly related to the success he is able to bring about.

---

[5]   John Gardner. *On Leadership*. (New York: Free Press, 1990), 2.

SECTION 12

TRUST, CONFIDENCE, AND PREDICTABILITY

"I trust everyone but still cut the cards."
Finley Peter Dunne

"Few things help an individual more than to place
responsibility upon him and
to let him know that you trust him."
Booker T. Washington

"What upsets me is not that you lied to me, but that from
now on I can no longer believe you."
Friedrick W. Nietzsche

"It is better to be defeated on principle than to win on lies."
Arthur Caldwell

Leaders tend to recruit and retain people who are predictable and trustworthy. We see it time and again as leaders (corporate heads, civilian government officials, and military officers) take key staff members with them when they move to new positions. Many times the hiring and transfer of staff is not necessarily due to competence but to predictability and dependability. Occasionally, I have seen simply adequate but trustworthy performers moved along by leaders when, in fact, better talent already existed within the new organization.

Leaders tend to adopt and promote people in whom they have developed trust and confidence. Trust and confidence are earned by people who are forthright and honest. Early on, the leader is evaluating everything he is told by a new employee. He wants to know—is this guy believable? Does he color the truth? Does he build himself up by sniping at his peers? Does he magnify his own worth by boasting? Does this guy exaggerate the good and play down the bad? When I ask for his opinion or recommendation, does he give me his unambiguous, unequivocal yes or no, concur or non-concur, or agree or disagree, and why? I don't want it sugar-coated, and I don't have time to figure out what he means.

According to Robert Ringer, "Another common form of lying that most people don't normally think of as lying is exaggeration. Nothing makes me lose confidence in a person more quickly than to discover that he inflates his facts or feats."

Deceit or deception may be the most hideous form of dishonesty. Hotel magnate, Conrad Hilton wrote that,

> Once you start it, there's no place that deception can stop—and of course it has to start with self-deception, even if it's only the self-deception of believing we can get away with it. True, sometimes we are not discovered. But all of modern psychology and psychiatry is based on the belief that our self-deceptions drive things into our subconscious where they make all kinds of trouble.

Alibis, excuses, and passing the blame are bane to trust and confidence. When trusted leaders mess up, they fess up. They realize that everyone messes up sometimes, so their competence is not in question (of course, repeated ill-advised and/or foolish mistakes will risk one's reputation for competence), but failure to own up puts one's credibility at risk.

Alibis, excuses, and passing the blame are bane to trust and confidence.

In his book, *13 Fatal Errors Managers Make*, Steven Brown describes *Internalists* as performance-oriented people, and those who hide behind alibis and excuses as *Externalists*. He claims that, "People fail in direct proportion to their willingness to accept socially acceptable excuses for failure." According to Brown, *Externalists* position themselves as victims while *Internalists* take the hand they are dealt and play it to the hilt.

To nurture trust and confidence in oneself, the leader:

- quickly owns up to errors, blunders, and lapses (don't we all make errors?)

- personally tells the boss of his blunders before someone else does

- accepts full blame and avoids alibis (even if partial blame belongs elsewhere)

- if at fault, accurately describes or slightly overstates the damage. Never fear, someone else will explain the real damage, and you may be vindicated while your credibility actually grows.

Exceptional leaders are always searching for people who are believable and predictable. They are looking for people who are believable and predictable *all the time*. Business and management expert and author, Robert Ringer tells us that, "All lies have one thing in common, and that's the price you pay when you're caught. And make no mistake about it, sooner or later you will be caught, which results in the most difficult of all losses to recoup—loss of credibility."

Exceptional leaders are always searching for people who are believable and predictable. They are looking for people who are believable and predictable all the time.

SECTION 13

A PREDOMINANT CHARACTERISTIC OF SUCCESSFUL ORGANIZATIONS

"Morale is the lifeblood of any team."
Pat Riley

"The failure to understand people is the devastation of western management."
W. Edwards Deming

"Equal opportunity for all; special privilege for none."
Zell Miller

Morale is the oxygen of the organization! Organizational morale, at any point in time, is directly proportional to the productivity of that organization. We have all seen organizations and teams floundering week after week and then suddenly, as a result of some stimulus that dramatically enhances organizational morale, do a complete turnabout, accelerating productivity exponentially. Sometimes the stimulus is a change in leadership, a change in leadership technique, the acquisition of another team member who is able to generate enthusiasm, or simply a change in the environment or challenge.

> **Organizational morale, at any point in time, is directly proportional to the productivity of that organization.**

For decades, leaders have recognized the importance of morale in the development of winning organizations. Napoleon is said to have stated, "Morale is to numbers as three is to one." That statement implies that morale is a significant success multiplier to the organization.

It's easy to build a case for the importance of organizational morale. However, it is difficult to understand why social scientists spend so little effort in examining its nature and characteristics. It seems that many educators would rather wallow in theory than in the science of motivation. So we continue to put our future leaders on the streets without the slightest perception of how to motivate their primary resource, people.

According to Admiral David Farragut in a letter to his son in 1864, "Remember also that one of the requisite studies for an officer is man. Where your analytical geometry will serve you once, the knowledge of men will serve you daily." The late Harold Geneen put it succinctly, "... I do not think business schools are wrong in teaching what they do, but I do think their emphasis is lopsided. Too much attention is being paid in those schools to the mechanics and not enough to the emotional values of good business management."

Successful leaders are students of the science of motivation. They read, digest, and understand the practical guidance offered by the late Peter Drucker, Warren Bennis, Mark McCormick, Norman Vincent Peale, and, yes, Pat Riley, Bill Walsh, and Mike Krzyzewski from the world of athletics. Whether we are talking about the secrets of George Patton, "Mad Dog" Mattis, or Nick Saban—the goal is the same, the development of winners through motivation.

Almost daily, I observe the failure of leaders to understand the ways and means of generating morale within the organization. Some years ago after observing my son's high school basketball team absorb another sound beating, the coach commented on the price they would pay in Monday's practice. In other words, the coach's motivation technique was to threaten and punish the team such that they would play harder next time. Occasionally, some players do need this type of motivator as a wake-up call. In this particular case and in many cases, the kids had played their hearts out and already felt punished enduring the loss itself. I submit that motivation techniques such as the above are usually counterproductive, affect player enthusiasm, and ultimately contribute to further losses. We've all observed techniques such as these in the work place, the classroom, and, unfortunately, on the Little League diamond. Often accompanying this technique are inflammatory remarks regarding the team or players' intestinal fortitude. This further denigrates the players' enthusiasm, nurturing resentment, distraction, and loss of focus; and, as is all so often in the case of youth athletics, a loss of the desire to ever participate in organized athletics again.

In all but the rarest of losses, leaders must accept their share of the blame and rally the team around the lessons learned and the next opportunity to win. Successful leaders do not dwell on losses. They realize that the goal is to get morale as high as possible as quickly as possible for the next event.

Years ago, after observing the proud Duke University basketball team suffer a shellacking at home at the hands of the University of Virginia, I listened to Coach Krzyzewski in his post-game wrap up on AM radio. It was clear to me how Duke had won back-to-back national championships. Thirty minutes after the game, Coach Krzyzewski was already accepting blame for the loss, putting the team's mind at ease as to blame, and preparing to tackle the following week on a positive note. There was no scapegoat, no threats, only positive encouragement, and make no mistake, the players heard what their coach said on the radio that night. And, as one would expect, they bounced back the following week with a crucial victory.

Successful leaders do not dwell on losses. They realize that the goal is to get morale as high as possible as quickly as possible for the next event.

In the world of athletics and in the military, I have frequently heard the old adage about hard work and discipline being the keys to success. There is certainly some truth to this adage. However, I believe that dogmatic adherence to this maxim, particularly by young inexperienced leaders, has done more damage to organizational morale and hence, success, than any maxim I can recall. The problem is that inexperienced and unlearned leaders can't discern when hard work and discipline turn into overwork and over-zealous discipline. Overwork and over-zealous discipline destroy enthusiasm, create dissension, and cause serious deterioration of performance. Show me a coach or military leader who boasts about how hard his practices or training exercises are and I'll show you a coach or military leader who rarely has a record of success worth boasting about. Good leaders recognize the limits of hard work and discipline and are able to achieve the training or work goals by challenging the team or work force without destroying the morale necessary to achieve success.

Overwork and over-zealous discipline destroy enthusiasm, create dissension, and cause serious deterioration of performance.

While on the subject of hard work and discipline, I want to tackle an associated error committed continuously in the field of athletics and the military by supposedly trained leaders attempting to maximize the performance of their players or soldiers. Through the years it has become crystal clear to me that over-training and conditioning are often more damaging to unit performance than under-conditioning. In an under-conditioned unit, the players or soldiers may tire more quickly, but in an over-conditioned team, not only are the bodily reflexes sluggish, but the body is also susceptible to injury. Furthermore, unit attitude, morale, and enthusiasm are low before the event even begins! According to the late Bill Walsh when he coached the 49ers, "We never scheduled more than two hard workouts in a row, because I wanted to make sure players did not become so weary that they were unduly vulnerable to muscle pulls, or that their only concern in practice was to simply survive." It's vitally important that players or soldiers take the field to learn something rather than to only have their courage tested. This approach should be reflected all the way down to the Pop Warner level. There are only so many times when a coach (or military leader) should test an individual's courage or willingness to totally sacrifice.

I once read an interview that a sportswriter conducted with Greg Maddux, the superb Atlanta Braves and Chicago Cubs pitcher and Cy Young Award winner. Maddux relayed how he felt tired and worn out all the time during the season. When asked how he counteracted this, he replied, "I don't do anything. I rest—especially in the last two months of the season. I'm not worried about being in shape, because I am in shape. I'm not worried about missing a running day. If my legs are shot, I won't run. I'm not going to go out there and feel tired and then run myself into the ground and get even more tired. I'll take the day off. I'll give my body a day to come back on its own."

> **Good leaders recognize the limits of hard work and discipline and are able to achieve the training or work goals by challenging the team or work force without destroying the morale necessary to achieve success.**

In many of the major blowouts in college and professional athletics, particularly in big games when the tendency is to over-prepare, I believe the culprit is over-training. You can sense it in the lack of quickness (a telltale sign of over-training), mental lapses, and lack of genuine enthusiasm in the losing team. There is simply no other reason why teams with superb credentials can be so soundly beaten. By the same token, I believe that many of the major upsets are accomplished by properly trained teams with *fresh legs*, mental sharpness, and enhanced enthusiasm against superior teams that have been over-trained and thereby, sacrificed their quickness, mental sharpness, and enthusiasm. Experienced leaders understand and practice common sense and some restraint in training their units. They know that failure to monitor training exercises or practices can undermine a unit's physical abilities and morale.

I am so convinced that morale is a major efficiency and capability multiplier, that I believe it must be planned. But who ever heard of a morale planning meeting? I believe there are times when morale meetings are in order. The successful leader recognizes the danger signals of deteriorating morale. He is always on the alert for unusual absenteeism, observed boredom, idle standing around, lack of enthusiasm, obvious reluctance to speak or converse with leadership/ management, gossip and rumors, or a downright sultry attitude. The appearance of these traits in any number is a sure sign of deteriorating morale and calls for a meeting with subordinate leaders and maybe even the work force as a whole. Whatever the method, the problem has to be tackled head-on and immediately.

Morale is a major efficiency and capability multiplier

Experienced and successful leaders sense the climate of the organization by getting out and talking to the unit or team members. According to former Brigadier General and author S.L.A. Marshall, "A common fault among young officers during World War II was to approach the troops with an attitude of condescension, intellectual separation, and priggishness." I saw this very trait in the Marine Corps among our young leaders educated at some of our more noted universities. Invariably, this lack of communication and failure to spot the danger signals cited earlier manifests itself in the morale and attitude of the unit. Moreover, once the problems begin to surface, the often young leader begins to search for the scapegoat or he criticizes the unit members. On the contrary, upon observing the danger signals, the leader must ask himself the question, "What am I doing wrong and how can I fix it?"

There exist a number of aphorisms, which are coincident with high morale in any organization:

- Individual morale is key to organizational or unit morale
- The actions of the leader are a primary ingredient of high or low morale
- Units with high morale are significantly more successful than organizations with low morale.

Tom Peters and Nancy Austin wrote that excellent companies are people-oriented. Caring is a part of the institutional culture. In *lip service* companies, management still talks to people, but the substance is not there. Caring executives do everything possible before laying-off competent and loyal workers. Their companies stand out as a result of their intense and persuasive concern for their work force. It is not hard to single out the leaders who sincerely care about the worker. They can be found out in the plant conversing, in the warehouse asking questions, and consistently searching for ways to better the lot of the worker.

Whenever I think of the caring leader, I am reminded of the passage in Donald Hankey's *The Beloved Captain* when he described how the Captain cared for his men after the foot march:

> We all knew instinctively that he was our superior—a man of finer fiber than ourselves, a "toff" in his own right. I suppose that was why he could be so humble without loss of dignity. For he was humble too, if that is the right word, and I think it is. No trouble of ours was too small for him to attend to. When we started marches, for instance, and our feet were blistered and sore, as they often were at first, you would have thought that they were his own feet from the trouble he took. Of course, after the march, there was always an inspection of feet. That is the routine. But with him, it was no mere routine. He came into our room, and, if anyone had a sore foot, he would kneel down on the floor and look at it as carefully as if he had been a doctor. Then he would prescribe, and the remedies were ready at hand, being borne by a sergeant. If a blister had to be lanced, he would very likely lance it himself there and then, so as to make sure it was done with a clean needle and that no dirt was allowed to get in. There was no affection about this, no striving for after-effect. It was simply that he felt that our feet were pretty important, and that he knew that we were pretty careless. So he thought it best at the start to see to the matter himself. Nevertheless, there was, in our eyes, something almost religious about this care for our feet. It seemed to have a touch of Christ about it, and we loved and honored him the more.

It has been said that tact is the lubricating oil of human relations. I suspect it has a significant effect on the morale of an organization also. The caring leader is thoughtful in his approach to correction. He is careful in how he offers suggestions to unit members such that they come across with the desired effect.

The following actions on the part of the leader lubricate the relationship between the leader and the members and have a significant impact on the morale of the organization:

- Giving verbal compliments
- Reprimanding judiciously, in private, allowing the subject to *save face*
- Putting the worker first; let him know that you think that he deserves the best pay and working conditions that the organization can afford to provide. Never pass up an opportunity to improve the lot of the worker.
- Believing that it's better never to make a promise than to break one
- Removing the minor irritants (lack of paper products in the bathrooms, inconvenient parking, standing in line, insufficient breaks or time for lunch, unserviceable furniture or equipment, etc.); and,
- Avoiding ridicule and cajoling at all costs.

There will always be those in the work force, the military, and the athletic business who believe ridicule and cajoling will motivate people to higher levels of performance. All leaders must understand that if an organization lacks drive, enthusiasm, and the desire to excel, ridicule and cajoling will not provide it.

One of the finest books on human relations ever written is *How to Win Friends and Influence People* by Dale Carnegie. Carnegie says, "Any fool can criticize, condemn, and complain—and most folks do." The leader's dilemma is how does he point out errors and shortfalls, particularly when they are repeated, without causing resentment, ill will, and morale deterioration? The effective leader does it by tactfully providing constructive criticism and convincing the unit that he sincerely cares about the welfare and upward mobility of the individual.

In conclusion, on what may be the most important section in this book, let me say that the morale of the unit or team is the essence of success, and I am reminded of a story told by a Baptist minister some years ago. According to the pastor, a Mennonite farmer explained that he had a horse that could pull 4500 pounds and another that could pull 4700 pounds, but together they pulled 12,000 pounds. This says much for the synergism of the team. Rudyard Kipling said it best in this great verse from his *Second Jungle Book*:

> Now this is the law of the Jungle—as old and as true as the sky; And the Wolf that shall keep it may prosper, but the Wolf that shall break it must die. As the creeper that girdles the tree-trunk, the law runneth forward and back; **for the strength of the Pack is the Wolf, and the strength of the Wolf is the Pack.**

SHAPING ATTITUDES

"There is real magic in enthusiasm.
It spells the difference between mediocrity and
accomplishment."
Norman Vincent Peale

"Productivity increases as managers increasingly
understand the human factor and effectively deal with the
attitudes, fears, motivational blocks,
and the phantoms that lurk within the minds of people."
Steven Brown

According to former U.S. Marine and author William Manchester, "I can denounce the Marine Corps and I frequently have. But so can lovers quarrel, and to those who have fought in it, the Corps is like the memory of an old affair, tinged with sadness and bitterness, yet with the first enchantment lingering. It is a mystique, wholly irrational; and right or wrong, a legion of men bred to logic will lay down their lives for its intangible honor tomorrow."

I know of no organization in western civilization that so shapes the attitudes of its people like the U.S. Marine Corps. But even after twenty-six years in this extraordinary outfit, I am not sure myself how it is done. I suspect that it starts with the Marine drill instructor. No Marine ever forgets his drill instructor. The drill instructor manifests perfection in appearance, attitude, demeanor, and competence. He or she becomes the ultimate role model. But it doesn't end there; the love and obedience to the principles of being a Marine seem to endure forever.

Who has ever observed a Marine in an airport terminal with his tie undone, his blouse unbuttoned, or his shoes dirty? Marines are erect in carriage, no nonsense in demeanor, and move about with confidence and poise. They represent the epitome of how leadership can shape the attitudes of the led.

Zig Ziglar and others have written that the subconscious mind works to complete the picture painted by one's desires. In his book, *Think Like a Winner*, Walter Staples tells us that, "positive thinking does not allow the 10 percent that is not perfect in your life to influence and control 100 percent of your thinking and day-to-day existence." Staples continues to say that the subconscious mind will influence one's actions, demeanor, and behavior to fulfill one's self-image; "The subconscious is always the obedient servant, the obliging slave to the conscious perception, and it is activated by mental pictures. But once it has received its instructions, it becomes the most powerful influence in your life." This helps explain the Marine mindset. Marines are what they are because they believe they are.

I am convinced that leaders can virtually will success and victory, but the mind must possess the right picture. We see it in athletics where the near impossible upset occurs, and we see it in other organizations when the will of the leader is so powerfully reinforced that the vision is realized. It is not about intelligence or intellect; it is much more than that. Some leaders have it and some do not.

> **Leaders can virtually will success and victory, but the mind must possess the right picture.**

I recall when I returned from the Haiti peace-keeping operation in 1995, I was asked by the president of Bridgewater College to return to my alma mater and serve on a search committee to seek a new football coach. One of the candidates was Jay Paterno, son of Coach Paterno. Possessing a Master's Degree from Penn State and being a follower of Coach Paterno at that time, I told Jay how much I respected his father's work and success. Jay's response was, "Yeah, but you didn't have to live with him." All I could think about was, "Is that what my grown children say about me?" Probably so.

Sadly, since the Jerry Sandusky abomination and the apparent cover-up, some question Coach Paterno's personal values. But I have some consternation about how the affair was handled by the Board and that they dismissed him without a hearing. He should have been given the opportunity to defend himself. In my judgment, the Board reacted to the media without allowing justice to be served, especially in view of what Coach Paterno had done for the university and its students for so many years.

I am sure many disagree, but I am disheartened that an icon of college football that shaped the attitudes of his players for many years has fallen from grace. However, I wonder what Coach Paterno could have been thinking; to report and follow up was a no-brainer.

SECTION 15

SELF-APPRECIATION IN THE WORKPLACE

"More than anything else, you and I seek self-esteem."
Steven Brown

"My mother's kiss made me a painter."
Benjamin West

Some positions, by their very nature, do not generate self-appreciation; hence, individuals filling those positions sometimes punch the time clock, extend their breaks, abuse their sick leave, and so forth and so on. They may be present for only a paycheck. The successful leader will find ways to elevate the pride and self-appreciation of these people. Changing the name of the job, giving supervisory or quality control responsibilities based on performance or time on the job, awards of recognition, and just plain verbal compliments may be helpful.

Another way may have nothing to do with the job itself such as sponsorship of after-work activities where employees can receive recognition other than on the job (heading the department bowling or softball team, successful participation in the company chess tournament, etc.). To maximize the employee's self-appreciation after such endeavors, the leader should publicize the activity and the results. At my last academy, we gave special name tags to employees with twenty years of service so others recognize their longevity on the job. Napoleon exercised this principle when he acknowledged how much a man would do for a little piece of ribbon to wear upon his uniform.

Social scientists argue that *empowerment* of the work force is consistent with worker self-appreciation. I hate the term as it is but a euphemism for delegating, but I agree with the concept.

Successful leaders authorize decisions at the lowest levels possible and accept the inherent risks. They are calling on the ranks for ideas and then implementing them. This bottom-up input is often successfully used in business development and strategic decision-making. If the social scientists want to call that empowerment, okay, but to me it is delegation of authority and common sense leadership.

Successful leaders authorize decisions at the lowest levels possible and accept the inherent risks.

SECTION 16

A WINNER'S CLIMATE

"Winning is not a sometime-thing here.
It is an all-time thing."
Vince Lombardi

Organizational climate is a term in vogue in today's business schools. Command climate is a popular term in the military. In either case, climate refers to the work environment of an organization as perceived by the workers, and, it is closely akin to morale. It can be found among the faculty of a school, the pilots of an airline, the coaching staff of a college, the sales force in a real estate office, or the ranks of a U.S. Marine rifle company. Many factors contribute to the organizational climate to include the work environment, the presence of cliques and *favorites*, the leadership style of a leader, the leader's genuine concern for his people, and the integrity of the unit's leadership.

Probably the easiest and quickest fix for a poor organizational climate is improvement of the work environment. Few realize that "part of being good is looking good." Workers appreciate a professional environment, one that is clean, orderly and with a decor consistent with a quality product. Everyone wants to be proud of where they work. They genuinely like to bring their families and friends to their work place if it represents something they are proud to show off.

Part of being good is looking good.

I'm reminded of a downeast North Carolina high school where litter was strewn throughout the campus, grass and shrubs were never

89

pruned, gymnasium bleachers were dirty, painting was long overdue, and the faculty appeared and acted indifferent towards the students. As one can imagine, student attitude was not conducive to learning. Attendance at school activities was demonstrative of the climate in that particular school. In my judgment, the organizational climate could have been improved significantly in one month of clean up, paint up, fix up.

The presence of cliques can have a deleterious effect on organizational climate. Cliques force the choosing of sides. Athletic coaches are very familiar with the dangers herein. Cliques can devastate a team. Even as a young twenty-three-year-old high school football and baseball coach, I was ever observant for the formation of cliques. I even assigned lockers with the elimination of cliques in mind. The same was true of room assignments and vehicle assignments when playing on the road.

Vince Lombardi was ever fearful of the danger of cliques. It has been said that, to minimize friction on the team, he deliberately made the players think of themselves as a unit, not as rookies and veterans, offense and defense, blacks and whites. Off the field, the players congregated in different groups, with a variety of interests, and cliques were minimized.

As stated above, cliques have an immeasurable negative impact on the climate of an organization. A leader's goal is for everyone to feel like an integral part of the team and not be left out. Cliques do just the opposite. They imply that some are in the *in group* and some are not. A leader strives to foster unity of effort and a positive attitude among all players or workers. If everybody is comfortable in the organization and feels as if they are contributing, less time is spent fretting about position, and a wholesome unity of attitude is established.

Cliques have an immeasurable negative impact on the climate of an organization.

The problem of cliques is exacerbated if the leader himself is in a clique within the organization. This happens when the leader is blatant in his selection of favorites. When it occurs, resentment and petty jealousy are fostered and the winners' climate deteriorates into a losers' climate. This type of clique can often be found on high level organizational staffs. The prudent leader is careful to keep even the appearance of such a relationship at bay.

The problem of cliques is exacerbated if the leader himself is in a clique within the organization.

In spite of the above, there is a tendency to have favorites due to similar interests, like personalities, personal appearance, etc., but effective leaders wisely control or effectively hide such tendencies to preclude even the perception of favoritism, because of the effect it can have on organizational climate. According to Coach Lombardi, "... he ceases to be a leader if he identifies too closely with the group. He must walk, as it were, a tightrope between the consent he must win and the control that he must exert."

Leaders must attack gossip and invective sniping head on. They refuse to participate in either, realizing that participation implies approval. Both are infectious and can seriously demean organizational climate and must be eliminated immediately when detected.

Leaders must attack gossip and invective sniping head on.

I possess an exacting mindset about how things are and how things should look in an organization as I am a firm believer that part of being good is looking good, however, I am aware of the dangers inherent in a fault-finding climate. The new student, player, soldier, or worker should not be initiated, trained, or oriented by constant verbal criticism or any form of punishment. The focus should be on progress, not failure. Steven Brown wrote that, "Countless trainers have approached the learner with a machete in hand, chopped out the weaknesses, and then watched the person to death in perfection. The training arena has no place for ridicule, sarcasm, or negative critique." The exception to the above may be in the early stages of military recruit training when the trained and experienced drill instructor informs the recruit of his or her indulgent, self-centered lifestyle that is inimical to success in a military unit destined for combat.

In his work on managerial behavior, T.L. Daniel wrote that, regardless of the name given to the leadership style, a style that focuses on the mission and goals and provides an environment conducive to worker participation in all aspects of the organization is the style that facilitates a positive organizational climate.

A team, a faculty, a military unit, a corporate work force, or a student body intuitively knows if there is a genuine care and concern for their welfare. Questions asked, things said and done, and body language, in the aggregate demonstrate the attitude of the organization towards its people. Real leaders seize the opportunity to mingle with the work force or team, ask the right questions, listen to the answers, and act where possible. They know how to exhibit care and understanding by visible actions that are for the benefit of the unit. Caring organizations invariably score high on organizational climate, and their level of achievement is consistent with this attitude.

Successful leaders understand the techniques necessary to create a winner's climate. Additionally, they recognize the telltale signs of a declining organizational climate and are quick to tackle the causes.

> **Leaders seize the opportunity to mingle with the work force or team, ask the right questions, listen to the answers, and act where possible.**

THE ENVIRONMENTAL SCAN

"The prudent leader is ever vigilant that the failure to
frequently scan the rapidly changing
environment is tantamount to defeat in time."
Jim Benson

An organization's environment refers to the external conditions that affect its strategy, market, and processes. Senior leaders must continually adjust the sails to the wind. These constantly changing conditions are a primary focus. The actions of the Environmental Protection Agency (EPA), for example, may have a major influence on everything from expansion of a business to the acquisition of materials necessary to run the business.

The location of a church, school, or business can aversely affect its longevity. A deteriorating location can damage the customer base or the traffic pattern in the vicinity of the business. Increasing crime in the area can significantly reduce the customer base. This is particularly true of restaurants and other businesses that require customers after daylight hours. This can be mitigated to some degree with well-lit parking areas and walkways.

Constantly changing technologies can introduce a new competitor almost overnight. Changes in society's view of the work force with regard to minority rights, women in the workplace, and the provision of mandated health care all influence the organizational environment. The company or corporate intelligence network may be a covey of lawyers who are the *eyes and ears* of the organization in terms of its environment. The executive leader is ever vigilant that the failure to frequently scan the rapidly changing environment is tantamount to defeat in time.

> **Constantly changing technologies can introduce a new competitor almost overnight.**

VISION AND THE ALL-CONQUERING WILL

"The will-to-win-to-be without equal,
is not particular in where it finds a permanent home."
LTG Hal Moore

"Vision is the art of seeing things invisible."
Jonathan Swift

"Where there is no vision, the people perish."
Proverbs 29:18

"Vision is compelling, even compulsive,
which is both the problem and the power."
Harrison Owen

"A man has made at least a start on discovering the
meaning of human life when he plants shade trees under
which he knows full well he will never sit."
Elton Trueblood

"There is no such thing as great talent without great
will-power."
Honore de Balgar

"He who is firm in will, moulds the world to himself."
Johann Goethe

So much has been written on the subject of vision and strategic intent that I hesitate to address it, but it is so integral to success that its omission would be an oversight. I have seen it defined in various journals as mission, philosophy, purpose, and beliefs. I take exception with each of the definitions. The *mission* is what an organization does to achieve the leader's intent or vision. It is the means to the end. The *vision,* simply put, is the leader's *desired end state* at some point in time. The *philosophy* and *beliefs* surrounding the vision are the guiding principles as to how the organization accomplishes its mission. Similarly, the *purpose* of an organization is its reason for existence.

In the past three decades, and to a large degree the result of worldwide recognition of the Edward Deming Theory of Management, strategic planning and the resultant creation of an organizational vision have become vogue. However, visionary thinking has been existent in successful organizations for centuries. For the non-believers, read Wess Roberts' description of how, in 451 A.D., Attila the Hun took 700,000 barbarians, gave them a common purpose, discipline and esprit, and marched through Eastern Europe at will, despite organized resistance by seemingly superior forces.

Contrary to popular belief, all leaders are *not* visionary leaders. My theory is that leaders possess varying degrees of visionary abilities. Likewise, all are not conceptual thinkers. Nor are all even effective vision implementers in their own right. The visionary leader is one who clearly sees the end state of the organization at some point in time—maybe five years, ten years, or twenty years out.

The conceptual thinker/planner is one who, when given the vision, sees and articulates the path to the end state. The implementer executes the plan. Ideally, the head of the organization (commander, president, or department head) would be a visionary who was previously successful as a planner with conceptual thinking skills. His operations officer would be a conceptual thinker who has also experienced previous success as an implementer. And, of course, the implementers would be the aggressive young lions capable of carrying out the operational plan devised by the conceptual thinking operations officer.

Unfortunately, abilities and jobs are often mismatched. If the head of the organization is not a visionary, priorities continually change, reorganizations are frequent, and the organization flounders. If the operations officer is not a conceptual thinker, hence, cannot view the path to the vision; then the visionary head of the organization is soon ready for therapy. And, if the young implementers are really visionaries who prefer to sit and think about how things ought to be rather than getting their hands dirty making things happen, chaos is presently knocking at the door or is already there.

The visionary leader is one who clearly sees the end state of the organization at some point in time—maybe five years, ten years, or twenty years out.

The head of the organization must provide the vision. All have seen examples in the field of athletics where a great assistant coach fell from grace once given the responsibilities of head coach. As an assistant, he was given the vision, could visualize the path, and implement the process. However, as the head coach, he lacked the ability to visualize the end state and the components thereof. Hence, it was not long before he was again an assistant and probably once more, a successful one.

During the American Civil War, President Lincoln had great vision, but until he appointed Ulysses S. Grant as overall commander, he was unable to find a General Officer who could comprehend his vision, conceptualize a plan, and see to its execution. The great leaders not only are visionary, but are able to articulate the vision to the unit and sell it as a recipe for success.

The great Chinese military strategist, Sun-tzu, demonstrated the point over 3,000 years ago that all men are not visionary when he said, "All men can see the tactics whereby I conquer, but what none can see is the strategy out of which great victory is evolved." The strategy, akin to the vision, was unknown to Sun-tzu's adversaries.

According to leadership author Harrison Owen, "Visionaries are typically driven people. In the vernacular, they see things that others don't see, march to a different drummer, and play by new rules." Jim Seybert reminded his readers in his *The One Year Mini for Leaders*, "The trouble with visionaries is that we see the ending before we get there. We don't pay much attention to details, so the last coat of paint doesn't always get applied." To me, these are not visionaries; they are dreamers.

There are those who perceive themselves as visionaries and merchants of change, yet have no strategic skills whatsoever. I am always suspicious of those whose so-called vision and reaction to every crisis is reorganization. To compound the problem, these are usually the same folks who seldom follow through to effectively see to it that management fully executes the change. They only create turbulence that invariably causes unexpected change within the organization that soon proves the reorganization a failure. Then the organization must endure the turbulence associated with reversing the change. Meanwhile, the rank and file wonder whether the drug urinalysis testing is aimed at the right group.

For those who possess visionary skills, they must be able to sell the vision to their constituents, demonstrate the competence to execute the actions necessary to implement the vision, and possess the force of will to see it through to completion notwithstanding the naysayers in their path.

> **I am always suspicious of those whose vision and reaction to every crisis is reorganization.**

We often hear the debate as to whether leaders are born or made, and consensus falls on the side of *leaders are born with appearance, aptitude, and tendencies to lead, but in the end; they are made*. However, rarely have we heard the same debate relative to visionaries. On this discourse, I fall on the side that says visionaries are imbued with an innate ability to clearly see the end state they seek.

Many lack the ability to paint the future of their organizations or even their own lives—someone else has to paint it for them. There are many leadership courses of instruction, and we can easily provide a program of instruction for future leaders; but who has ever seen or developed a program of instruction designed to develop visionaries?

The final piece of the visionaries' make-up is what the French call *élan vital* or the *all-conquering will* to see the vision through to completion. Others may use a softer description such as resolve or unwavering intention. With some level of assurance, we can measure one's intellect, strength, and speed, but we cannot measure one's heart or *will* to succeed, and it is more important than all of the others. Thus, it is insufficient to lead effectively and to visualize the end state—the great ones *will* it through to completion.

> The human WILL that force unseen,
> The offspring of a deathless sow,
> Can hew a way to any goal,
> Though walls of granite intervene.
> Be not impatient in delays,
> But wait as one who understands,
> When the spirit rises and commands,
> The gods are ready to obey.
>   James Allen, *As a Man Thinketh*[6]

With some level of assurance, we can measure one's intellect, strength, and speed, but we cannot measure one's heart or will to succeed, and it is more important than all of the others.

Those born with strategic vision, an unshaken will, and the force of personality to see the vision to completion are unstoppable. They appear to possess energy and determination often unobserved in others. They are purposeful in all that they do and when they say they are going to do something, it will be done. They are cognizant of the minefields in their path that include criticism, love of ease, indolence, dread of change, and jealousy. Oliver Wendell Holmes captured the essence of the will of man when he wrote, "Only when you have worked alone—when you have felt around for a black gulf of solitude more isolating than that which surrounds the dying man, and in hope and in despair have trusted to your own unshaken will—then only will you have achieved."

---

6   James Allen. *As a Man Thinketh.* Thomas Nelson Publishers (Nashville), 2009

Those born with strategic vision, an unshaken will, and the force of personality to see the vision to completion are unstoppable.

SECTION 19

THE HARD STUFF AND THE SOFT STUFF

"Honesty is the first chapter of the book of wisdom."
Thomas Jefferson

"Concentration is my motto—first honesty, then industry,
then concentration."
Andrew Carnegie

"I hope I shall always possess firmness and virtue enough to
maintain what I consider the most enviable of all titles, the
character of an honest man."
George Washington

"Women and wine, game and deceit, make the wealth
small, and the wants great."
Benjamin Franklin

Organizations that are founded upon and operated according to a set of values that encourage honesty, morality, integrity, and trust are invariably successful, respected, and justified. On the other hand, organizations that operate and make decisions from a position of deceit and self-interest frequently experience marginal success and instability within the work force. Former CEO of Levi Strauss & Co., Robert Haas, stated in an interview in the *Harvard Business Review* that,

We always talked about the hard stuff and the soft stuff. The soft stuff was the company's commitment to our work force. And the hard stuff was what really mattered, getting pants out the door. What we've learned is that the soft stuff and the hard stuff are becoming increasingly intertwined. A company's values—what it stands for, what its people believe in—are crucial to its competitive success. Indeed, values drive business.[7]

People expect more of their leaders than they expect of themselves. They assume that leaders are men of integrity who base their daily decisions on a strong foundation of values. When they cease to believe this, problems surface with the stability of the work force. Dishonesty, injustice, unfair business practices, and deceit are all contagious. If they exist at the top, they will exist to some degree throughout the organization. When they exist throughout the organization, failure is imminent.

A successful leader realizes that to be respected within the organization, he has to be respectable. Respect is earned by demonstrated competence, character, and integrity. Peter Drucker wrote that, "By themselves, character and integrity do not accomplish anything. But their absence faults everything else."

Dishonesty, injustice, unfair business practices, and deceit are all contagious.

Small dishonesties can become habitual. I'm reminded of the ten-year-old boy who asked his father what the word "ethics" meant. The father said, "It has to do with telling the truth." For example, if I go to the bank to cash a check and the bank teller, by mistake, gives me $100 too much; I then have an ethical dilemma: Do I tell your mother that I have the extra $100 or not?

Sir Walter Scott penned, "What a tangled web we weave, when first we practice to deceive." It is incredible what a chain reaction

7   Robert Haas. "Values Make the Company," Harvard Business Review, September, 1990.

a single white lie can ignite. It is troublesome in a family, but in an organization, it can be disastrous. Abraham Lincoln knew the danger inherent in lies when he said, "No man has a good enough memory to make a successful liar."

Spin is now the politically correct term for deceit. In recent years, spin, deceit, and dishonesty have become synonymous—*and* acceptable—in politics. I first recall the term during President Bill Clinton's administration. It was almost comical how that administration could spin the facts until they had new meaning. Today, both parties have mastered the technique to the point that I have a disdain for politics in general and many politicians. When I associate the deceitful words and actions of politicians in Washington, D.C., with the generous appurtenances of their offices, I understand why congressional approval ratings hover around 10 percent. Moreover, I appreciate the words on a plaque in the Rockefeller Center, which represent John D. Rockefeller's Credo: "I believe in the sacredness of a promise, that a man's word should be as good as his bond, that character, not wealth or power or position, is of supreme worth."

SECTION 20

GITTEN 'ER DONE

"He that leaveth nothing to chance will do few things ill, but
he will do very few things."
George Savile, Marquess de Halifax

"He who is outside the door already has the hard part of his
journey behind him."
Dutch Proverb

"When it's all said and done, more is said than done."
Lou Holtz

"The people who do great things in this world are
those who drive past the first layer of fatigue."
William James

There are those who spend their lives falsely appearing confident and composed, notwithstanding the fact that nothing is getting done. I call it *profiling*. Others flail about with their *hair on fire*, making everything appear to be a crisis. Somewhere in between there exists the *rational achiever* who knows when to react, recognizes a true crisis, responds accordingly, and continually gets the job done.

There is another type who is the consummate *prioritizer*. He prioritizes every task. Whenever he is asked the status of a project, he uses his priorities as his excuse for not having the project completed. I am convinced that one can prioritize oneself into mediocrity.

> ## I am convinced that one can prioritize oneself into mediocrity.

According to Darren Hardy in his fine book, *The Compound Effect*, "the early morning and evening hours are the bookends of our days. So much can be planned, done, and learned if we use those hours productively. Productivity during these times requires a good alarm clock, the self-discipline to set and mind it, informed prioritization, and the will to resist social media, mindless T.V. programs, on-line gossip, texting, and the scourge of video games."

The effective leader keeps all the *balls in the air* and will invariably show progress across the spectrum of his responsibilities. He is an expert at knocking out the easy ones while showing progress on the harder, long-term projects. The person who lists and performs all tasks in order of importance is the guy who takes two weeks to complete a twenty-five-minute task, because he prioritized it behind those tasks requiring sixty hours to complete. This individual has no idea how to manage his work and is destined for something less than mediocrity.

> ## The person who lists and performs all tasks in order of importance is the guy who takes two weeks to complete a twenty-five-minute task, because he prioritized it behind those tasks requiring sixty hours to complete.

But there is the master of *gitten 'er done*. He has an eye for and a low tolerance for idleness or anything akin to it. He senses when others are procrastinating or are unsure of the next step. This is the leader who "fixes things that are broken, corrects things that are bad, and changes things that are wrong"—without ever being told. By the grace of God, every organization should have at least one.

> ## This is the leader who "fixes things that are broken, corrects things that are bad, and changes things that are wrong"—without ever being told.

John Wesley, founder of the Methodist Church, was the antithesis of a procrastinator. A small and frail man of 5 feet 4 inches, each morning he arose at 4:00, delivered his first sermon at 5:00, and was on the road to the next one at 6:00. Each day he traveled sixty to seventy miles on horseback, preaching to anyone who would listen. At night he wrote books by candlelight and prepared his sermons and hymns. He pushed himself until he died at eighty-seven, respected and loved by thousands. John Wesley was a master of the art of gitten 'er done.

After returning from Vietnam, I was one of only six Marines in a class of 220 Army Captains at the Infantry Officers Advanced Course at Fort Benning, Georgia. We were studying battalion and brigade offensive tactics—specifically the frontal assault (frowned upon by my Army classmates), the envelopment, and the penetration. The six Marines in the course took a lot of good-natured ribbing from our Army classmates who claimed we knew only one offensive maneuver—one they called *hey diddle diddle, right up the middle*. In retrospect, there may have been some truth to their claims, and as I look back, that isn't a bad tactic in business either. *Hey diddle diddle* is one way of *gitten 'er done* and a classic example of the KISS philosophy (keep it simple, stupid).

Hey diddle diddle right up the middle is one way of gitten 'er done and a classic example of the KISS philosophy (keep it simple, stupid).

JUST DO SOMETHING

*"… young leaders become servants of what is
rather than shapers of what might be."*
John W. Gardner

"Doing nothing is the invisible mistake."
Rosabeth Moss Kanter

"Stuff happens to you, and there is stuff you happen to."
Anonymous

Nowhere is failure to take the initiative more important than on the battlefield. Most of us are aware of the frustrations President Lincoln experienced in his efforts to find a general officer who would seize the initiative. Probably his greatest frustration came with General George McClelland. Loved by his men, superbly trained, and seemingly offensive in style, he became the "splendid hesitator." And then there was General Meade who failed to pursue General Lee after success at Gettysburg, allowing Lee to cross the Potomac River and extend the war. Finally, there was Grant, admittedly not a tactician, but one who knew the value of the initiative and the objective.

In the U.S. Marine Corps, we tend to neglect teaching the defense. Of course, we teach the troops how to dig a foxhole, set up a perimeter defense, and how to plan and fire a final protective fire. However, the majority of our time was spent practicing how to attack from the sea, from the air, in the mountains, in the desert, and in the cities. I believe that is what has made the Corps what it is today, an aggressive offensive force, focused on defeating the enemy, not protecting itself.

In the work place, as on the battlefield, the winner is one who seizes the initiative, who is on the attack, and who possesses a bias for action as described by Peters and Austin in their highly acclaimed book, *A Passion for Excellence*. We see this initiative in many forms. We see it in the military officer or company manager who seizes upon a collateral duty that no one before him even touched. We see it in the new secretary who, without being told, completely reorganizes and dramatically improves the company files.

In the work place, as on the battlefield, the winner is one who seizes the initiative, who is on the attack, and who possesses a bias for action.

According to American writer and philosopher, Elbert Hubbard, "The world bestows its big prizes in money and honors for but one thing, and that is initiative. And what is initiative? I'll tell you; it is doing the right thing without being told." On initiative, business author, Mark McCormick writes that, "The projects people take on that are not part of their job description, which have not been assigned to them, are those projects for which people get the most recognition." Over the years, I have learned to recognize, acknowledge, and reward employees who consistently do what is expected of their position—and then some.

We have all seen senior leaders who have a propensity for studying proposals to death. They suck the lifeblood out of winners. But the effective leader can make impatience an art form with his action bias. Someone has termed this action orientation as *Ready-Fire-Aim*, which simply means *do something now*. Some leaders initiate task forces, project centers, quality circles, ad-hoc committees, and other short-term action teams to achieve progress and orchestrate change. These organizations are seldom found in the organizational chart, and the membership is usually composed of those *who don't have the time*. However, in organizations such as these with the right membership, members are not constrained by job descriptions, organizational charts, or authority conflicts. They are given a task, a standard, and a timeline to *get it done*. They can be successful if their mindset is *to maximize in lieu of compromise*. Of course, the larger the task force, the greater the tendency to seek compromise, which often achieves the ordinary or something less than excellence.

> **Over the years I have learned to recognize, acknowledge, and reward employees who consistently do what is expected of them in their position—and then some.**

Realizing that I tend to disparage compromise and consensus, I know that the two are not always evil and that to move forward the two are sometimes necessary. However, my caution is with those who compromise too soon on critical factors and those who seek consensus to share the accountability.

The aggressive leader overcomes the stasis through action and seizure of the initiative. He surfaces in the organization because of his action bias, persistence, and commitment. He is easily distinguished from cautious naysayers who avoid risk and seek the security of *further study*.

> **The larger the task force, the greater the tendency to seek compromise, which often achieves the ordinary or something less than excellence.**

In today's market, you can't just *be*; you must *perform* or you are gone. The best leaders create a sense of urgency within the organization. If there is no crisis, they may create one, because they know that crises create stress and anxiety that produce adrenalin; adrenalin produces energy; and energy produces results.

> **Crises create stress and anxiety that produce adrenalin; adrenalin produces energy; and energy produces results.**

In today's market, you can't just be; you must perform or you are gone.

In his autobiography, Colonel Joshua Chamberlain of the famous 20th Maine Regiment at Gettysburg wrote that his father had but one retort to young Joshua's "how do I do it" queries—"Do it, that's how." I love it!

SECTION 22

FAILURE IS OFTEN ACCEPTABLE

"There is a crack in everything—that's how the light gets in."
Leonard Cohen

"The surest way not to fail is to determine to succeed."
General William T. Sherman

"The way to succeed is to double your failure rate."
Thomas J. Watson

"We are failures-at least all the best of us are."
Sir James M. Barrie

Much has been written about how contemporary companies value failure and the acceptance of risk. In fact, one could conclude that failure is valued if in the name of initiative. In my research of the literature, I found nothing negative about failure! I am a believer in change and fully realize that the bold approach can lead to failure on occasion and, therefore, some failure has to be tolerated if an organization is to be forward leaning. However, we must not lose sight of the fact that repetitive failure will get you fired, and there must be some link between the failure and *healthy* aggressiveness. Failure that reflects stupidity, poor judgment, or poor execution will please no one.

One could conclude that failure is valued if in the name of initiative.

It would not be accurate to say that top executives hail failure, but they certainly recognize the benefits from it. They often view a failure as an opportunity to use it as a *springboard* to reach higher goals. Since all learning involves some failure, Bennis and Nanus in their fine prose in *The Strategies for Taking Charge*, have surmised that reasonable failure is a prerequisite to success and should be perceived as so by modern managers. And, after all, sometimes it is the cracks in our performance that let the light in, according to poet Leonard Cohen.

A former Johnson & Johnson director, the late Jim Burke, is quoted, "Any successful growth company is riddled with failure, and there's just not any other way to do it .... We love to win, but we also have to lose in order to grow."

Since failure is inevitable and in many cases a prerequisite to success, the leader must prepare the organization for it. This is particularly true in athletics, and I appreciate the late Coach Bill Walsh's analogy.

> When a wild beast or zebra is finally entrapped by the lion, it submits to the inevitable—its head drops, its eyes glaze over, and it stands motionless and accepts its fate. The posture of defeat is also demonstrated by man—chin down, head dropped, shoulders slumped, arms hung limply. This posture is often visible as players leave the field in the later stages of the game when things are going against them. I often brought this to our players' attention using that example from nature, and we became very sensitive to it .... I would assert, even in the most impossible situations, stand tall, keep our heads up, shoulders back, keep moving, running, looking up, demonstrating our pride, dignity and defiance.[8]

So failure is often an unwelcome accomplice to success but can be the very springboard that permits success at a level never anticipated. Strong leaders take failure in stride and press on. They often advance in the pursuit of success in a new direction. It is their implacable intent

---

8   Building a Champion: On Football and the Making of the 49ers." (New York), 1991

and purpose not to merely operate the organization but to advance it to a position it has never realized before.

Failure is often an unwelcome accomplice to success but can be the very springboard that permits success at a level never anticipated.

According to former U.S. Senator and Governor of Georgia, Zell Miller, "Life is a struggle to wrest success from the odds favoring failure and to achieve the satisfaction of overcoming the spiritual and physical challenges that confront the individual striving to be all that he can be, striving to make the world a better place for his loved ones of today and his descendants of tomorrow."

SECTION 23

IN ORDER TO WIN, LEARN HOW TO DEAL WITH DEFEAT

"Fearful are the convulsions of defeat."
Winston Churchill

*"Being defeated is often a temporary condition. Giving up is
what makes it permanent."*
Marilyn Vos Savant

Losing and failure can be the impetus to greater success if the leader prepares the organization for the eventuality. Similarly, failures must be acknowledged and analyzed, and the lessons learned shared within the organization. We learn from our mistakes. Successful organizations—and their effective leaders—learn what they can from the failure and then move on. Usually little can be gained by dwelling on "the pathogens."

Whether in the workplace, on the athletic field, or battlefield, the prudent leader early on prepares the organization for its first setback. Otherwise, the membership may experience a mental letdown after the defeat leading to sniping, finger-pointing, and grumbling that will surely affect the future in ways never anticipated. This is often demonstrated in athletics when a team gets off to a robust start and an enviable winning streak, but subsequent to the first loss, ends up losing four or five straight games. It becomes apparent, in these instances, that the coaches have not prepared players for the first loss and that the rest of the season is still ahead of them. It is a leader's responsibility to ensure that a loss or failure of an initiative does not turn into a tailspin.

> **It is a leader's responsibility to ensure that a loss or failure of an initiative does not turn into a tailspin.**

Former editor of the *Harvard Business Review*, Rosabeth Moss Kanter, has written ground-breaking books related to corporate success and failure. Maybe the most thought-provoking was her treatise on how winning streaks and losing streaks begin and end, entitled *Confidence.* The thesis of her book is that winning and losing are not episodes but trajectories. They are tendencies, directions, and pathways. Ms. Kanter emphasizes that losing can cause future poor performance just as winning can be the purveyor of future wins. Losing can create loss of confidence, which creates doubt and all kinds of challenges for the future that include under-investing, self-pity, and other losing reactions.

> **Losing can cause future poor performance just as winning can be the purveyor of future wins.**

It is the leader's imperative to prepare the organization for setbacks that can easily turn into losing streaks and the eventual demise of the organization. This is particularly notable in combat and athletics subsequent to having one's nose bloodied in a firefight or on the gridiron. The effective senior leader understands the human condition after failure and prepares the organization for such a set back before it occurs.

SECTION 24

CONFORMITY AND RISK AVERSION

"Our doubts are traitors, and make us lose the good we oft might win, by fearing to attempt."
William Shakespeare

"When you can't make up your mind which of two evenly-balanced courses of action you should take, choose the bolder."
General W. J. Slim

Conformity is as much a symptom of fear of change as jaw pain is to an abscessed tooth. Conformity or copy-cat strategies are the safe course of action, but they rarely win championships. Good leaders recognize the dangers of conformity.

Most *success practitioners* advocate change, but little is said about the necessity for speed in initiating change. Rapid changes require rapid decision-making—yes, decision-making that is not laden with study after study and staff paper after staff paper. Rapid change results from streamlined staffing, clear and concise decision papers, and staff presentations to the decision-makers that are to the point, convincing, and without bias.

Perfection is the enemy of rapid change. Successful leaders do not suffer those who resist and encumber changes for the sake of the status quo or the lack of executive courage. Not only do successful leaders appreciate change makers, but they seek employees who possess the flexibility to recommit quickly when someone else initiates rational and informed change.

> **Rapid changes require rapid decision-making—yes, decision-making that is not laden with study after study and staff paper after staff paper.**

I reserve the right to discriminate against those who are satisfied with the status quo, who are bound to the ways of the past, and who resist change solely because it involves risk and means work. They become enamored with the "way we have always done it" and resist the policy and procedural changes required to create growth and value. Bill Pollard, the insightful former CEO and Chairman of the Board of the highly successful ServiceMaster Company wrote, "The leader who makes things happen through others must learn to dip, upset, and redirect these activities of difference …." Conformity is the antithesis of required and rational change that leads to growth and success.

But change-minded executives must not be naïve for in every profession there are pathogens (trouble-makers) who will undermine them, especially if they are successful. Yes, even in our pugnacious military where integrity is considered a core competency; there are the left-brainers who will torture every idea or plan for change. That said, there is a need for left-brained analysts who prevent hair-brained, hip-shot changes.

I have seen it time and time again executive leaders who seem to exist in perpetual crisis. It makes little difference what the occupation or the nature of the business. There is often internal crisis, external crisis, or self-made crisis that accompany change.

> **Yes, even in our pugnacious military where integrity is considered a core competency; there are the left-brainers who will torture every idea or plan for change.**

The internal crisis exists because of employee relations, reductions in expenditures, modifications to employee benefits, plant equipment casualties, workforce reductions, policy or procedural modifications, and more. The external crises may relate to supplier issues, customer relations problems, communications, new environmental regulations, or product failures.

Finally, there is the self-made crisis wherein the executive leadership creates a sense of urgency to awaken a seemingly lethargic workforce. The executive courage and force of will that often creates internal tension and disrupts the feel-good homeostasis, will often kick-start the organization when sales and margin have taken a dive and alibis are prolific. Sometimes it takes a perceived crisis to silence the naysayers who may want to stop or slow the right-brain visionary.

> **The executive courage and force of will that often creates internal tension and disrupts the feel-good homeostasis, will often kick-start the organization when sales and margin have taken a dive and alibis are prolific.**

According to Dr. Robert Khayet, former Chancellor at the University of Mississippi, "Many people want progress, but very few want change. This is true even if change is a clear improvement." Organizations that are wedded to the status quo are often destined for the boneyard. Nothing can save them except new leadership, which is sometimes necessary throughout the organization.

In summary, leaders must anticipate organizational resistance to change. Moreover, they must recognize its normality. When resistance exists to the extent it becomes unhealthy for the organization, the pathogen(s) must be terminated.

> **When resistance exists to the extent it becomes unhealthy for the organization, the pathogen(s) must be terminated.**

SECTION 25

THE UNREASONABLE MAN

"The reasonable man adapts himself to the world;
the unreasonable man persists in trying to adapt the world
to himself.
Therefore, all progress depends on the unreasonable man."
George Bernard Shaw

Admiral Hyman G. Rickover, father of America's nuclear Navy, stated,

> The deepest joy in life is to be creative. To find an
> undeveloped situation, to see the possibilities, to
> decide upon a course of action, and then devote the
> whole of one's resources to carrying it out, even if it
> means battling against the stream of contemporary
> opinion.... [9]

We are all aware of those who, when confronted with a seemingly valid request for change, immediately begin to look for reasons why the change won't work. On the contrary, leaders should look for the positives first. They must look for the benefits of a new way of doing business rather than looking for possible consequences to the change. Machiavelli, in *The Prince*, stated, "There is nothing more difficult to take in hand, more perilous to conduct, or more uncertain in its success, than to take the lead in the introduction of a new order of things."

According to Steven Brown in his *13 Fatal Errors Managers Make*, "The need for creativity runs through every segment of business. Management is essentially a 'thinking job, not a doing job.' The

---

9   http://www.wikipedia.ord/wiki/Hyman_Rickover

123

lifeblood of any organization lies in ideas and creative thinking." Yet, invariably, the creative individual invites jealousy and resentment along with sniping, gossip, and criticism. Therefore, to create or advocate change, one has to be courageous. The leader must prepare the battlefield for this resistance by building consensus before he springs his plan. Timing is critical. He knows that his chances for success are much higher if he is able to acquire support from some of the *movers and shakers* within the organization prior to publicly proposing his plan of action.

Resistance to rational change is not a new phenomenon. Attila the Hun, the barbaric but innovative Chieftain who reigned around 430 A.D., had a methodology for dealing with resistance:

> We cannot expect to change our long-held traditions, to reorganize our army and to create great cities without internal opposition. Among you chieftains and Huns will be those whose spirits cling to our past ways. We will show patience with you unenlightened ones. Yet, if you choose not our new cause and cause dissension, you will be stricken from our ranks.[10]
> Wess Roberts

Change is inevitable. It is often the maverick who has the executive courage to advocate dramatic change. Yet, the maverick is often shunned and unpopular. He is often viewed as a "loose cannon" or an irrational and unreasonable person. According to George Bernard Shaw, "The reasonable man adapts himself to the world; the unreasonable man persists in trying to adapt the world to himself. Therefore, all progress depends on the unreasonable man." The leader should cherish the ideas of the maverick who should be listened to and encouraged to express his ideas. Change is a natural order within the unit; not change for the sake of change and not politically-motivated change, but change for the sake of progress. Stasis is the enemy of rational change and hence, progress. The leader with courage is an agent of change and will endure

---

10   Wess Roberts. *Leadership Secrets of Attila the Hun.* (Grand Central Publishing, New York. 1990).

criticism and resistance in order to forge ahead and achieve victory within and for the organization.

Stasis is the enemy of rational change and hence, progress.

SECTION 26

MARKING TIME

"Do not sleep, lest you come to poverty;
open your eyes, and you will be satisfied with bread."
Proverbs 20:13

"Heck, by the time a man scratches his behind,
clears his throat, and tells me how smart he is,
we've already wasted fifteen minutes."
Lyndon B. Johnson

"In truth, people can generally make time for what they
choose to do;
it is not really the time but the will that is lacking."
Sir John Lubbock

More and more, I am recognizing the value of time as a resource. Time is discussed to some degree in the next section on procrastination, but I believe a few thoughts on time as a resource are in order. Ben Franklin noted, "If time be of all things the most precious; wasting time must be, the greatest prodigality." Franklin also wrote that, "Lost time is never found again; and what we call time enough always proves too little."

Englishman John Mallory explained that marginal performers rarely take work home or work in places and at times not specifically designed for work. Working in the airport would never occur to them. Others realize that if all administration is saved for the office, little time will be left to get out and about to view, hear, and sense the heartbeat of the organization. Hence, the effective leader seizes every opportunity to accomplish the administration of his position.

He takes work home; he works in airports; and when he can find someone else to drive, he prepares while traveling from one meeting to the next.

Effective executives are masters at managing their time. They know that their discretionary time is limited; and most of it will be spent keeping the organization running efficiently. Additionally, they avoid practices that waste the time of their subordinates such as overstaffing that seems to promote interacting rather than working and holding an excessive number of meetings that reflect a dysfunctional organization.

How leaders use their time has become the topic of much research. David Novak, Chairman and CEO of Yum! Brands, Inc., wrote about the difference in activity (feel good stuff) and action (moving the needle stuff). He emphasized how leaders often spend too much time on the feel good stuff (clearing out the email, preparing reports, and schedule correspondence) and not enough time on actions that affect the bottom line. The problem can be exacerbated by the paucity of white space in the daily routine that would permit the solitude required to think through work priorities and focus on actions that move the needle towards the true objectives of the organization.

Zig Ziglar cautions that "… time is generally wasted, lost, stolen, misplaced, or forgotten in minutes not hours." Have you ever noticed how few idle people there are in the first class or business section of an airplane? These are the people who know the value of time, have used it efficiently, turned it into success, and, yes, often it means a seat in the front section of the airplane.

Marking Time is a military term used to describe marching without moving forward or back. In other words, the feet go up and down but the soldier or Marine remains in place. *Marking Time* well describes an organization led by an ambivalent, indecisive executive. Either he goes out, or the organization goes down.

Marking Time well describes an organization led by an ambivalent, indecisive executive. Either he goes out, or the organization goes down.

SECTION 27

SOMEDAY ISLE

"Deadlines are the mother of invention."
John M. Shanahan

*"Once men are caught up in an event, they cease to be
afraid. Only the unknown frightens men."*
Antoine de Saint-Exupery

*"You don't hold your own in the world by standing on guard,
but by attacking and getting well hammered yourself."*
George Bernard Shaw

"All glory comes from daring to begin."
Eugene F. Ware

*"There are 190 ways to get beat, but only one way to win;
get there first."*
Willie Shoemaker

Many procrastinate on decisions, because they want more information;
they procrastinate on actions, because they fear the risk. I call these
people *thinking procrastinators*. But there exists another group of
procrastinators who fail to act because of apathy or lethargy. This group
is hopeless in any discourse on success and succeeds only by accident
because of the efforts of the subordinates of the procrastinator.

Successful executives possess an instinct that tells them when
enough information is available to make a decision and an inner
confidence that permits them to act in spite of fear of failure. They

know that tomorrow is not as good as today, and when nothing is gained today, something is lost tomorrow.

> **Successful executives ... know that tomorrow is not as good as today, and when nothing is gained today, something is lost tomorrow.**

Procrastination is a crippling disorder and a frequent cause of failure. Its repercussions include stress and anxiety, which exponentially decrease one's chance for success. There are dozens of reasons to wait but few are legitimate. People most often procrastinate due to fear and doubt, lack of focus, distraction, and lethargy. Zig Ziglar wrote that, "Someday Isle (someday I'll) is a non-existent island. Someday Isle is one of the greatest excuses ever given. Tomorrow is the greatest labor-saving device ever brought to light."

What is it about youth that inherently includes a healthy measure of procrastination? The attitude that, "eventually I will feel like accomplishing this task or doing my homework" is a loony tune that has to be exorcised. In actuality, one finally starts the task when the pressure and anxiety rise to the point where one is urged into action. But it doesn't have to be that way. Zig Ziglar put it as well as I've heard: "Don't wait until you feel like taking a positive action. Take the action and then you will feel like doing it." It is true, once we start the action, the progress itself motivates us to see it through.

My experience has been that a *do-it-now* leader is invariably successful. Under the right circumstances, impatience can be an art form. I have zero patience for procrastination and no matter the scenario, if one *what ifs* the downside or pejorative consequences, they are almost always minimized by early implementation. Furthermore, quick implementation beats the competition to the punch. Catching up with the competition is a real challenge. If we implement first, the competition has to react to our implementation (no matter how imperfect), while now we are already focusing on product improvement. It's like going on the offensive and seizing the initiative. We never give our competition time to figure out how to beat us, because his time is consumed in catching up.

Some have called it the *do it now* mentality, *paralysis by fear*, or the *hurry sickness*. They claim that it is a disease that produces stress, unhappiness, and affects longevity. A compulsive drive to beat the deadline, keep all the balls in the air, stay in the fast lane for promotion, and carry the day can be counter-productive if completely unreasonable and not balanced with exercise, a stable diet, and rest. However, to the astute leader, tomorrow exists only in the *long range* plan. All else is action, and action requires a *do it now* mentality. Tomorrow may be an organization's single greatest impediment to success.

> **Tomorrow may be an organization's single greatest impediment to success.**

Lance Corporal King (left) in Quang Nam Province, South Vietnam. King was the "best point man" I ever observed

Left to right, Reverand Bob Richards, Twice Gold Medal Olympian, yours truly and Couch Ray "Spizzerinctum" Bussard (See Section 57) at Bridgewater College. These are two of the greatest competitors I have ever known. I told them both, "They should have been Marines."

*Mary Benson and son Jimmy at the President's Quarters
at Marion Military Institute.*

*Captain Paul Butcher, C.O. USS. Oklahoma City presents
musket to Captain Benson. 1975.*

Son Jimmy and daughter Catherine
at Marion Military Institute.

Left to right, grandson Ross, daughter Catherine, yours
truly, and grandson John at Riverside Military Academy

"You Can, You Will, You Must Succeed !"

Attributed to Coach Ray Buzzard
University of Tennessee

*Howard and Holly Kalmenson, Jim and Mary Benson in
the Kalmenson's beautiful home in Hollywood Hills, CA*

21-Sept -2015
To Colonel James H. Benson, USMC (Ret.). In special
thanks & appreciation for then - LT Benson's bravery and
humility in risking his own life to recover the bodies of
my friends, Paul Dukes (LA) and Mickey Hooks (KY),
Scout/Snipers, 1st Marines, Republic of Vietnam, KIA
31-August-1969, Quang Nam Province.
Semper Fidelis _____
Bob Depp, S/S, 1st Mar, RVN, 1969

Jim Benson at Riverside Military Academy

Catherine Benson (daughter) in Panama

RVN On/about 7-Aug-'69
Cpl Paul Dukes - KIA 31-Aug-'69
Minden, LA

On/about 5 Aug-'69
Cpl Paul Dukes - (Left) KIA 31-Aug-'69
Pfc Marshall - (Middle back)
Pfc Bob Depp - (Right)
Republic of South Vietnam

Left to right, Carlos Cervantes, Juliette Turner,
Actress Janine Turner, Jim Benson and Mary Benson
at Riverside Military Academy.

RVN On/about 7-Aug-'69
Scout Sniper L/Cpl Mickey Hooks - KIA 31-Aug-'69
Princeton, KY

Mary Benson
"The fairest of the fair"

*Commemorative brick that that was placed at the U.S.
Marine Corps Museum in Quantico, VA*

*Marine scout/snipers Paul Dukes (left) and Mickey Hooks
(right) were killed in action on August 31, 1969 in Dodge
City (appropriately named by Marines), Quang Nam
Province, Republic of Vietnam. These were the heroes
whose remains were recovered by "Doc" Hargett and
2nd Lieutenant Benson as discussed in Section 7. Picture
provided by scout/sniper Bob Depp who was severely
wounded that same month. Bob is a true friend in arms.*

SECTION 28
THE WALLENDA FACTOR

"Boldness becomes rare, the higher the rank."
Carl von Clausewitz

*"Doubters do not achieve; skeptics do not contribute;
cynics do not create."*
Calvin Coolidge

Winning is perpetual and so are winners! Those who expect to win, win, and continue to win. Those who spend their time trying not to lose are making the bed for their next defeat. Stonewall Jackson admonished his staff to "Never take counsel of your fears." Surely, General Jackson did not advocate reckless thinking without thought to the consequences. The great General was simply a believer in the initiative and understood the dangers of self-doubting and hesitation.

American authors, Bennis and Nanus wrote of the "Wallenda Factor" and how shortly before Karl Wallenda fell to his death in 1978, he had been obsessed with the thought of falling and had taken extra precautions before that fateful 75-foot high-wire walk in San Juan, Puerto Rico. One might conclude that Wallenda had predestined his fall with his pre-occupation with not falling. On this one occasion, he took counsel of his fears to a degree never before observed in him by others. To the contrary, General Marshal Foch wrote to General Joseph Joffre in 1914, "My center gives way. My right recedes. The situation is excellent. I shall attack."

In conclusion, effective leaders create their own destiny by their proactivity while losers suffer a fate by their reactivity.

Effective leaders create their own destiny by their proactivity while losers suffer a fate by their reactivity.

SECTION 29

HEADACHE OR HERO

"The race is not to the swift or battle to the strong, nor does
food come to the wise or wealth to the brilliant or favor to
the learned; but time and chance happen to them all."
Ecclesiastes 9:11

I shall never forget Private Dewey. When I arrived in South Vietnam in June of 1969, fresh out of Officer Candidate School (OCS) and after completion of infantry training at The Basic School, I was assigned as 2nd platoon commander, Company I, 3rd Battalion, 1st Marine Regiment, 1st Marine Division. I was excited and proud to be assigned to the legendary 1st Marines. After briefings at regiment and battalion, I was driven in a jeep to join my company. The company commander gave me a quick briefing on the company area of operations (AO), and 1st Lieutenant Eric Shaefer, executive officer, took me down to meet the platoon sergeant and to join the platoon as they were leaving in thirty minutes to establish a platoon patrol base about ten kilometers from the company command post.

As soon as 1st Lieutenant Shaefer departed, the platoon sergeant explained standard platoon procedures to include order of march, introduced me to the right guide and squad leaders, and finished his brief by saying, "We are only taking two beers per man." The platoon sergeant had been acting as the platoon commander for about five weeks as the previous platoon commander and ten or so other Marines in the platoon had been killed in an intense fire fight with well-trained North Vietnamese regulars in an area appropriately called Dodge City.

I was not your typical new twenty-two to twenty-three-year-old 2nd Lieutenant. A former high school football and baseball coach with a Master's Degree, I was twenty-six and more mature and confident than most newly commissioned lieutenants. As I quickly assessed the platoon sergeant's pronouncement relative to the beer, I concluded that the platoon looked to be forty to forty-five Marines and two beers per man equated to eighty to ninety beers, and we were going out for seven days to find and kill Viet Cong! Thus, my first order as a Marine Officer was, "Get the *expletive* beers out of the packs." With a look of disdain, the platoon sergeant gave the order.

Walking #3 in the column as we departed the company area, I observed the actions of the point man carefully and was impressed how he moved by bounds, took appropriate security halts, used hand and arm signals effectively, and avoided trail intersections. The point man's name was Private Dewey. Regardless of rank, the point man in an infantry column makes multiple decisions with little time to weigh his options. The patrol is going to follow him in whatever route he chooses. Hopefully, he is chosen for his experience and mature decision-making. Normally, the patrol leader, whether officer or enlisted, does not walk point because of the inherent dangers of booby traps, etc.

Private Dewey was wounded two or three times in his action-filled tour of duty but never so seriously that he could not return to the field. Dewey was sometimes described as a *train wreck*. He must have hated water, because even when we had the rare opportunity to bathe, he would find a way to disappear. Bathing was usually washing down in a nasty stream bed with clothes on—that way the Marines got their bodies and clothes clean at the same time. Moreover, no one wanted to risk being shot at in the nude.

Daily hygiene expectations also included brushing of teeth and shaving. Dewey always seemed to need a shave. His squad leaders got their butts chewed out more over Dewey's appearance than anything tactical. Dewey was the Marine you wanted to keep out of the platoon picture or during the commanding officer's periodic rifle and personnel inspection. However, Private Dewey was the first to volunteer for the most dangerous missions. Notwithstanding his hygiene issues and inability to stay awake on watch when in a night perimeter defensive position, we all respected him; we knew he would be there when the shooting started.

Because of casualties, the platoon numbers could dwindle to the high twenties; so when occupying a platoon patrol base away from the company, manning the perimeter at night was arduous and conducting daytime patrols and night ambushes left little time for sleep. We were normally required to send out two to three ambushes a night and a couple of listening posts, so the perimeter was manned by the remaining Marines (the ambushes and listening posts were sometimes all night and at other times for a set number of hours so they could be coming and going all night).

We changed platoon positions every other night and dug-in (foxholes) each time. Normally, we had two Marines per foxhole, and they manned the foxhole at night in shifts. In essence, each Marine had a daylight combat patrol, a night ambush or listening post (ambush sites were considerably farther from the patrol base than listening posts and for obvious reasons, were composed of more Marines), and a period standing night and day watch at his foxhole.

There was never enough sleep, so sleeping on watch (and in ambush sites and listening posts) was a continuous security issue for the platoon. Private Dewey could sleep standing up, so there was little hope he would stay awake on watch at night. Where in previous wars, one could be summarily shot for sleeping on watch; such punishment was unheard of in Vietnam. However, punishment existed, and it was handled by the platoon sergeant and squad leaders. Dewey occasionally had so much swelling around his eyes, I often couldn't tell if it was his normal face contour or if he had been *disciplined* again. To his credit, he never alibied or complained to me.

One late afternoon, while in a bridge security position with the company (we had just returned from seven days at a platoon patrol base), I received an order from then company commander, 1st Lieutenant Shaefer, to mount up, conduct a movement to contact, cross the Son Cu Dee River, and set up a blocking position as another company swept the area the next morning and, hopefully, drove the Viet Cong towards our blocking position. It was the kind of mission we liked except for the river crossing part. I had never done a platoon-size river crossing before, and there were no boats. Moreover, we didn't want to conduct the river crossing at night, so we had better haul-ass (the trails in this area of operations were replete with booby traps, so movement to the river would be tenuous in the necessary "hurry up" mode). When I received the order, 1st Lieutenant Shaefer advised me that the 3rd Platoon's point man had been killed in the same area a week or so before.

I prepared a fragmentary order (FRAGO) to save time, and as we formed up in column making last minute equipment and ammunition checks, 1st Lieutenant Shaefer, who was rightfully a stickler on camp discipline and cleanliness, walked up and said to me, "Your platoon area looks like a shithouse; get back and clean it up." I wondered if he had ever made a night river crossing right next to a known VC hamlet. Nonetheless, we executed the cleanup, got away late, and took the additional risk by moving too quickly with virtually no security halts, and by the grace of God arrived at the river at dusk without detonating any booby traps.

We selected a crossing site at the narrowest point we could find, checked the river depth (it was too deep to wade), and made final preparations determining who could swim and who could not. We selected the best swimmer to swim the rope across and anchor it. I sent Lance Corporal Engleman (a courageous twenty-year-old 3rd squad leader) to the rear of the column to retrieve the rope from whomever had been assigned to bring it.

I became anxious as Engleman did not return as quickly as he should have. Just as I was about to go back down the column of squads to see what the hold-up was, I saw Engleman moving forward with PVT Dewey in tow, and Engleman was clearly not happy. As he approached, he quietly (we were tactical) said, "PVT Dewey was assigned to bring the rope, and he doesn't have it." I reacted and hit Dewey across the face with an open hand and was surprised how loud it was. Officers do not strike enlisted men, and it was the only time I did it in my twenty-six years in the Corps. I can only describe Dewey as subdued and remorseful (later when my anger subsided, I was remorseful also that I had struck one of my men). Later, when I contemplated the incident, I realized that 1st Lieutenant Shaefer had interrupted us during our equipment checks to go back and police our platoon area, and surely we would have discovered Dewey's mistake had the checks been completed. But what do we do now that we are at the river without a rope?[11]

---

11   1st Lieutenant Eric Shaefer was a gungy, mustang (former enlisted Marine) lieutenant. He had been wounded twice, had won a Silver Star for heroism, and was a good company commander.

Some Marines carried inflatable rubber sleeping mattresses (the troops called them rubber ladies) that I had planned to load with equipment and move the radios, packs, helmets, flak jackets, and heavy weapons across the river, but I did not trust the rubber mattresses to carry all of the gear and have Marines hanging on the sides as they paddled across the river. The Viet Cong used sampans to move up and down the river, and since we were near the hamlet, I sent a fire team north and another south to look for one or more. The team moving towards the hamlet found two submerged sampans and returned with them in short order. While we were organizing the order of crossing, troops were blowing up their inflatable mattresses.

It was now dark, and I used the sampans to send a fire team and a machine gun squad across first to establish security at the far bank. The crossing was incredibly slow and tense. Some of the Marines were poor swimmers or non-swimmers, especially in their uniforms and boots (no one wanted to take their boots off in this extremely dangerous scenario) and did not want to cross without a rope. I gave them the options of staying on the near bank alone or crossing with the platoon. They agreed to cross and if they had not, we would have bullied them across, but I hoped to avoid the commotion. It was about 2330 when we got all men and equipment across and married up with their gear. We were wet, stressed, and exhausted and too tired to go far (noise discipline was poor, which was typical when the troops were tired), and it was too late and dark to be particular about the site to set in for the night.

I had two choices: one was to set up the platoon perimeter in the middle of a rice paddy with a dense tree line on each side, or two, set up in one of the tree lines—neither was good.

Moving into the tree line at night caused control problems, and the Viet Cong could crawl up close and toss grenades into the perimeter as they had done previously at another area called Go Noi Island. Moreover, even though it was now early morning, we had to dig foxholes for protection, and it was easier to dig in the rice paddy. However, no concealment existed in the rice paddy, and the rice paddy dikes offered the only cover.

I decided to set up in the middle of the rice paddy and put two-man listening posts (LPs) out in the vicinity of each tree line. Once the LPs were briefed and in place, we set out claymore mines around the perimeter, and established the watch (one man up and awake at each foxhole and the radio watch established). I gave the platoon sergeant the first command post (CP) watch, and I laid down hoping to get a few hours of sleep so that later I could take the early AM radio watch and work on my order for the mission the next morning.

The problems began about 2:00 a.m. when one of the LPs called in that they had movement behind them (this meant that movement was between the LP and our position!). We awakened everyone and went on 100 percent alert. Since the LP was only about 100-150 meters from our perimeter defense, the movement was close to our lines, but no one in our position heard the movement. There was never a doubt that the VC were aware of our presence and had observed our activities. The near hamlet and others close by were clearly VC inhabited although the fighters were rarely observed during daylight hours.

We were in a pickle, because the LP could not fire (not their mission either) for fear of shooting back into our perimeter, and we could not fire (on some rare occasions, we would "recon by fire") for fear of hitting the LP, which was not dug in.

At first morning light, the LP returned to our position, and we were all puzzled by the activity so close to the perimeter of our defense, but no other enemy action had occurred. The LP had done its job; it detected movement and gave us early warning causing the 100 percent alert. However, when Lance Corporal Earl and others went out to bring in the claymore mines that they emplaced around the perimeter the night before, Earl found one that had been turned around so that if he activated it, it would have exploded into the perimeter. We could only surmise that the VC had, with great stealth, crawled sapper-like past the LP and close enough to the perimeter to turn the claymore around—talk about testosterone! My assumption was that the Marines on watch were asleep and never heard the movement even when we went to 100 percent alert. The VC probably intentionally made enough noise for us to fire the claymore at our own perimeter, but the Marines on watch in the vicinity of the claymore were all asleep, thus saving their own lives.

We could only surmise that the VC had, with great stealth, crawled sapper-like past the LP and close enough to the perimeter to turn the claymore around—talk about testosterone!

After a night including a treacherous river crossing, a 100 percent alert beginning at about 2:00 a.m., pegged tension and adrenaline flow, we had a C-ration breakfast and coffee with double sugar for wakeup. But the VC were not the only resourceful unit in Quang Nam province that day. At first morning light, we would do a visual reconnaissance of the area around our patrol base looking for a vantage point, usually in a nearby tree line. I then employed the tactic of having a four-man killer team depart the bivouac site about twenty minutes before the platoon moved out.

In what I would describe as cunning and guile, we would make something of the team's departure knowing that the VC were watching us. Moreover, we would do a less-than-perfect job of burying our C-ration trash, knowing that once we were gone the VC would visit our patrol base and ransack the trash for left behind food, ammunition, and equipment as some less-disciplined units would do on occasion.

As the platoon moved out of the patrol base, the four-man killer team would have carefully doubled back and set up a sniper-like ambush to kill the VC who came into the patrol base in search of useful litter. The main body of the platoon would take a security halt about 200-300 meters out of the patrol base and wait for the killer team to return with or without bounty.

Sure enough, we heard the multiple cracks of the M-16 and M-14 rifles as they laid a volume of fire on the two VC that had entered the camp in search of left behinds. With two kills to account for the morning, the killer team took off on a non-tactical retreat to meet up with the platoon. We were easy for them to find as we fired a green star cluster pyrotechnic to signal our position. The four-man killer team was made up of two Marines for near security and two shooters. The teams were normally volunteers whom I trusted because of their experience and courage. On this day once again, PVT Dewey was a volunteer and one of the shooters.

Even the battalion commander knew PVT Dewey. On another day, we were on a battalion-size sweep well south of Hill 37, which was the battalion command post. The battalion commander had sent an ultimatum to the company commanders relative to weapons safety, apparently in response to another accidental discharge in the battalion or regiment. On this particular late afternoon after humping about twelve kilometers in a column of companies (the companies were in a variety of formations), my company was entering the battalion perimeter for the night bivouac. I noticed the battalion commander talking to the battalion S-3 (Operations Officer). As the S-3 gave our company commander his sector of the perimeter using the clock system (e.g., Company "I" occupy 0600 to 0900), we began movement into the perimeter.

Standard operating procedure was to unchamber all rounds (ammunition) before entering the perimeter. As my first squad was entering the perimeter, I heard and saw the accidental discharge of an M-79 grenade launcher (blooper, as it was called) and as the round bounced past the battalion commander and the S-3 Officer, I expected to hear the explosion at any time. Instead the round lay dormant on the ground, inert, as its flight was too short to acquire sufficient revolutions and air time to arm. I can only assume that the battalion commander was so glad to be alive that he and the S-3 officer simply ordered the companies into position and called for the engineers to destroy the round. In a moment, I knew who had the blooper accidental discharge; it was Dewey. I was the responsible officer and assumed that I would have my heels locked in front of the battalion commander in due time. I never heard a word about it.

One might ask why Dewey was carrying the M-79 blooper in the first place. Each squad had a grenadier who carried the blooper, and I assume his squad leader made him the grenadier, because he was seemingly fearless. The blooper was normally an indirect fire weapon, less accurate in a direct fire mode, and rarely used at close range. However, on another occasion, Dewey's squad (he was not the squad leader) took fire from a hamlet, and upon observing a VC shooter on the run, he fired instinctively; the round hit the VC in the back of the head—end of VC.

The final Dewey episode that I shall describe is related to a company–sized search and destroy operation northwest of Hill 55, which was the location of the regimental command post of the 1st Marines.

It was mid-morning, and my platoon had been the point platoon for about two hours when the company commander moved us to drag (rear security) behind the weapons platoon. We usually rotated the duty of point platoon as it was very tense duty especially in this area of the badlands. As the other companies moved through us, and we were now in the rear of the column of platoons, the company halted, and I walked forward to speak to the weapons platoon commander. Normally and rightfully, my radio operator would have stayed with me, but on this occasion he sat down, and I didn't say anything to the contrary.

Suddenly, the weapons platoon and my platoon came under heavy automatic weapons fire. I immediately went to the ground and crawled into an old mortar round indentation (about the size of a small child's inflatable swimming pool), and was joined by Lance Corporal Glenn Meadows from my point squad. The indentation wasn't big enough for both of us so we became real friendly. Without my radioman (Corporal Strickland, as I recall), I was out of touch with the company commander but was sure he was calling back to find out what was going on. I knew we had to get up and face the fire, but we needed some fire suppression and concluded from the sound of the AK-47s that the fire was coming from our right front at about our two o'clock. I could hear my platoon sergeant barking orders but could not make them out.

The rounds were flying right over Meadows and me and breaking the elephant grass that concealed us to a degree. I yelled back, "Machine gun up." To my surprise, considering how sporadic our return fire was and the volume of the incoming fire, I heard the rattle of the ammunition can (machine gunners carried their ammunition in its cans to reduce corrosion and for cleanliness)—no Poncho Villa bandoleers across the chest in our battalion. Lying on my back and looking up, I saw only a leg and a boot as it struck me in the stomach, then moved to kick me in the face. I heard the machine gun, ammo can, and a body crash to the ground as I gasped for breath. Momentarily, I heard the rat-a-tat-tat of the M-60 machine gun and with that my Marines were up firing and heading for the tree line. As I struggled to my feet to join the assault, I realized that PVT Dewey was the machine gunner who had run over me but was now the hero whose immediate response to my call for the gun was the difference maker.

Dewey's courage in a firefight was unbounded. Notwithstanding the headaches he could cause, he was a hero, and we were all grateful that he was on our team. When his tour was complete and just before he departed for the U.S., I promoted him to Private First Class (PFC) in front of the entire platoon. I have never seen such a celebration for promotion to PFC.

Dewey's courage in a firefight was unbounded. Notwithstanding the headaches he could cause, he was a hero, and we were all grateful that he was on our team.

On the gridiron of life, we cross paths with many whose actions and persona cause reason for admiration and affirmation. PFC Dewey remains special for me, because he made mistake after mistake but never lied or alibied; he took his punishment without a word. But when you needed a volunteer for a dangerous mission, Dewey wasn't looking down at his bootlaces. He was looking you right in the eye and without a word, saying "Pick me, sir." PFC Dewey was a Marine I shall never forget.

But when you needed a volunteer for a dangerous mission, Dewey wasn't looking down at his bootlaces.

SECTION 30

DRIVE

"If you start to take Vienna—take Vienna."
Napoléon Bonaparte

"The surest way not to fail is to determine to succeed."
General Richard Sheridan

The great sprinter, Eric Liddell, wrote that, "The secret to my success over the 400 is that I run the first 200 meters as fast as I can. Then, for the second 200 meters, with God's help, I run faster."

Call it drive, steadfast determination, commitment, fixity of purpose, grit, heart, or will, it makes little difference; but it is the personal characteristic that has more to do with winning and success than any I know. Talent, intelligence, tact, knowledge, personal appearance, contacts, and opportunity are all important and contribute, but none are as important as the insatiable drive to succeed

I have observed it in the classroom, on the athletic field, in combat, and in the business community; During the past twenty-five to forty years, there have been many success stories wherein Vietnamese immigrants have come to this country with little or nothing other than the desire and will to take advantage of any opportunity available. With language barriers, little capital in most cases, few contacts, and no transportation, they have worked and saved until they could open their own businesses. Subsequently, they have poured their hearts and minds into their endeavors, reinvested the profits, and achieved greater success than their native-born counterparts. Likewise, their children graduate from our finest universities with superior academic standing. What is their secret? It is simple; they possess the persistent determination to succeed.

Personal characteristics that many leaders seek in prospective employees are evidence of *drive*, commitment, persistence, and initiative. Evidence of these characteristics is seldom discernable from a resume. That is why written references are so important. If drive or persistence is going to show up, the reference is where it will be. The wise executive requires written references (or previous performance evaluations, if available) before he hires an employee for a key position. Former supervisors are less willing to be disingenuous about a prospect's work ethic, achievement, or character in a written narrative than verbally. An employee or player with drive will usually also have an exemplary work ethic, commitment, and insistence on excellence in all that he does.

It has become vogue to criticize the "wannabe's" in today's society. Not me. I'm quick to respond, "Give me all the 'wannabe's' you can find. I'll take them all, for they are the 'gonnabe's' of tomorrow."

Give me all the 'wannabe's' you can find. I'll take them all, for they are the 'gonnabe's' of tomorrow.

Not only do successful leaders possess superior drive, but they are always on the lookout for others, with the incessant determination to succeed. U.S. Marine Corps General Butch Neal of Gulf War fame once told me, "I recognize winners because they have a fire in their gut."

President Calvin Coolidge said, "Nothing in the world can take the place of persistence. Talent will not; nothing is more common than unsuccessful men of talent. Genius will not ... the world is full of educated derelicts. Persistence and determination alone are omnipotent. The slogan 'press on' has solved and always will solve the problems of the human race."

It is easy for one to become addicted to success, but who wouldn't be since success is the gateway to acclaim and affirmation. But there is a price to pay for acclaim and affirmation, and many are unwilling to pay that price. I have heard folks say that, "I would love to play the guitar like the late Jimi Hendrix or sing like Alison Krauss," but most would not possess the commitment to the practice, rehearsals, peaks and valleys, and disappointments that are preludes to such success.

> **It is easy for one to become addicted to success, but who wouldn't be since success is the gateway to acclaim and affirmation.**

> There's no thrill in easy sailing when the skies are clear and blue, there's no joy in merely doing things which anyone can do.
> But there is some satisfaction that is mighty sweet to take, when you reach a destination that you thought you'd never make.
> Spirella[12]

The recipe for personal or organizational success, seasoned with persistent energy and drive, initiative, and executive courage will consistently create exceptional outcomes on the gridiron of life.

---

12   Ted Goodman, ed. *Forbes Book of Quotations: 10,000 Thoughts on the Business of Life.* (New York: Black Dog & Leventhal Publishers, 2016)

SECTION 31

PRESS ON, REGARDLESS

"When everyone is against you, it means that you are
absolutely wrong—or absolutely right."
Albert Guinon

"It's a little like wrestling a gorilla.
You don't quit when you're tired,
you quit when the gorilla is tired."
Robert Strauss

"No deposit—no return."
John Naber

"For all your days prepare, and meet them ever alike.
When you are the anvil, bear—when you are the hammer,
strike."
Edwin Markham

Probably the most persistent individual I ever met was the former skipper of the U.S.S. Oklahoma City back in the mid-1970s. Captain Paul D. Butcher, U.S. Navy, was a former West Virginia school teacher and seaman recruit who rose to the rank of Vice Admiral in the U.S. Navy. As the Captain of the U.S.S. Oklahoma City, flagship of the United States 7th Fleet, Captain Butcher was a taskmaster. His favorite phrase was "Press on, regardless," and that is just what he did. He failed selection to flag rank three times before making Rear Admiral (one star) but then pressed on to Vice Admiral (three stars), where he commanded the Military Sealift Command and played a major role in transporting and resupplying U.S. forces in Saudi Arabia and Iraq during Operations Desert Shield and Desert Storm.

In my judgment, Vice Admiral Butcher was the epitome of persistence. Were this great American alive today, he would undoubtedly second Paul's challenge to the Philippians when he said, "But one thing I do: Forgetting what is behind and straining toward what is ahead, I press on toward the goal to win the prize." (Philippians 3:13-14)

It has been said that, "Those who fail in life often pursue the path of least persistence." It is troubling that many of our young people choose the easiest school, the easiest major, and the easiest professors. Never mind what their talents are or what profession they are equipped for; their goal is just to get that sheepskin! They under sell themselves rather than pressing on toward a challenging goal. We see it in the workplace as well. Many workers strive for a position of less responsibility, easier hours, or less pressure.

Fear of failure, resistance to hard work, and a preference for "free time" are all contributors to this mentality. Where are the entrepreneurs who went bankrupt two and even three times before they made their mark? In life, when nothing is gained, something is lost. Leaders and managers must recognize those who are truly committed and reward them. We must reward initiative, persistence, extraordinary drive, and uncommon achievement.

In my youth, I was dismayed over the luck of the prosperous. It seemed the same coaches year in and year out got the break that permitted another championship. The same well-to-do businessman owned the seemingly worthless property that the new shopping center would be built on. It was years before it became abundantly clear that luck is the residue of diligence, and those who claim they never get a break wouldn't know an opportunity if it jumped out and mugged them.

General Ulysses S. Grant preached that, "In every battle there comes a time when both sides consider themselves beaten, then he who continues the attack wins." At Chancellorsville, General Lee claimed to be "too weak to defend, so I attacked." This is the type of persistence we need to beat the opposition in today's markets, gridirons, and battlefields.

Rudyard Kipling captured the essence of persistence in two verses of his famous poem entitled *If*:

> If you can make one heap of all your winnings
>   And risk it on one turn of pitch-and-toss,
> And lose, and start again at your beginnings
>   And never breathe a word about your loss;
> If you can force your heart and nerve and sinew
>   To serve your turn long after they are gone,
> And so hold on when there is nothing in you
>   Except the Will which says to them: "Hold on!"
>
> If you can talk with crowds and keep your virtue,
>   Or walk with Kings—not lose the common touch,
> If neither foes nor loving friends can hurt you,
>   If all men count with you, but none too much;
> If you can fill the unforgiving minute
>   With sixty seconds' worth of distance run,
> Yours is the Earth and everything that's in it,
>   And—which is more—you'll be a Man, my son!

Press on, regardless!

SECTION 32

PROMIDENCE

"Man proposes, but God disposes."
James Robertson

*"I do not know beneath the sky nor on what seas shall be
thy fate;
I only know it shall be high, I only know it shall be great."*
Richard Hovey

*"Many are the plans in a man's heart, but it is the Lord's
purpose that prevails."*
Proverbs 19:21

*"Providence has at all times been my only dependence, for
all other resources seem to have failed us."*
George Washington

As I think and write about the leader's courage and the requirement to get out front (walk point), I am moved by my lack of understanding how faith and providence impact the end state of leaders' work. Clearly, there is a plan for us, and I suspect the Almighty places us where we are best suited, in time.

As a good Presbyterian, I believe that there is divine providence and power that sustains human destiny. I can't explain it, but I know it's there. I have seen it time and time again.

There have been many times in my life where events or opportunities appeared that could not have evolved by chance. I have no idea how many times I have gone to the Book of Proverbs when I was down or needed guidance, and what I was seeking was right there waiting. Even that is providential.

I believe that there is divine providence and power that sustains human destiny.

One of the foremost occurred in the Republic of the Philippines in 1972. In those days, there were several thousand United States military officers at the San Miguel Communication Station, Subic Bay Naval Base, and the large Clark Air Force Base. It had been decided that U.S. and Philippine dignitaries would conduct a Memorial Day wreath-laying ceremony at the tomb of the unknown soldier at the huge U.S. military cemetery in Manila to honor those Americans who had died in the Pacific in World War II.

Through some process unbeknownst to me (a young first lieutenant recently returned from Vietnam), I was selected to be the commander of the honor guard for that occasion. Few knew that my father had been killed in the Pacific during World War II, and the relevance of me being the honor guard commander that day had not dawned on me. However, as the honor guard was formed and the drums quietly began to play just before the appointed hour, the U.S. Ambassador, the U.S. base commanders, Philippines military leaders, and Colonel John H. Keith, Jr., commanding officer of the Marine Barracks at Subic Bay where I was stationed at the time, walked from the magnificent marble wall toward the honor guard and wreath at the monument for the unknown soldier. Colonel Keith and the dignitaries veered slightly to the right and upon reaching my position, Colonel Keith spoke to me. He said, "Jim, did you know your father's name is on that marble wall?" As he joined the other dignitaries, the reality and emotion struck home. My father remains an "unknown" who died in the South Pacific and whose remains have yet to be identified, and I was the honor guard commander as the wreath was laid on the tomb that ceremonially honored my father. These events could not have occurred by chance, and I still get cold chills thinking of that remarkable day.

James Robertson, the great pioneer, Revolutionary War hero, and Scotch Presbyterian, believed that there existed an "over-ruling mind" that governed human affairs. He felt that the providential purpose of his life was to walk point in the settlement of the western frontier. His story is beautifully told in Edmund Kirk's *The Rear-Guard of the Revolution.*

I am reminded of Conrad Hilton's experiences as he struggled in the early years in building his unprecedented hotel empire:

> And each time the walls were about to close in and crush me, when there was no light for even one step ahead, 'something' happened—a bellboy thrust his life savings into my hand, a difficult business rival took everything I had with one hand and gave it back with the other, a promise that meant my business life was broken by one man and seven others stepped in to fill the breach. Could I take credit for personal cleverness in things like that? I could not. To me, they were answered prayer.[13]

Colonel Joshua Chamberlain, the great Commander of the 20th Marine during the Civil War, President of Bowdoin College, and later Governor of Maine, may have said it best:

> But what it is, I can't tell you. I haven't a particle of fanaticism in me. But I plead guilty to a sort of fatalism. I believe in a destiny—one, I mean, divinely appointed, and to which we are carried forward by a perfect trust in God. I do this, and I believe in it. I have laid plans, in my day, and good ones I thought. But they never succeeded. Something else, better, did, and I could see it plain as day, that God had done it, for my good.[14]

---

13   Conrad Nicholson Hilton, *Be My Guest.* (New York: Simon & Schuster, 1957), 150.

14   Alice Rains Trulock, *In the Hands of Providence: Joshua L. Chamberlain and the American Civil War.* (Charlotte, North Carolina: the University of North Carolina Press, 1992), 219.

SUPERVISION AND OVERSIGHT – A PRELUDE TO SUCCESS

"An organization does well only those things the boss checks."
General Bruce Clark

"The eye of the master will do more than both of his hands."
Benjamin Franklin

One thing successful leaders understand is that they don't get paid for giving orders. Probably one of the most significant weaknesses in American management is the misconception concerning giving orders. Many feel that they are paid to see what needs to be done and tell others to do it. I submit that less than 50 percent of the leader's salary is for recognizing what needs to be done and directing someone to do it. The remainder is for *ensuring* that the job is done and done to standard. I once heard Army Lieutenant General Sam Wilson say, "In God I trust, everything else I check." Yes, the leader must be a supervisor supreme. He is always observing, overseeing, and, where necessary, correcting. He knows that to walk by a problem is tantamount to endorsing it. Even where trust is high, supervision must exist; but it is a coaching style of supervision.

> **He knows that to walk by a problem is tantamount to endorsing it.**

The main job of managers is to ensure that the vision and intent of the executive leadership is being carried out. How many times have we seen the well-conceived long-range plan gather dust as soon as it comes off the press? The senior leader must ensure that plans are implemented and that someone is assigned to supervise implementation. In fact, part of the plan should be an implementation plan to report progress at appropriate times to leaders or managers.

The military learned decades ago that futility is the lot of most orders without supervision. Additionally, unit or department feedback is frequently not dependable, because no one wants to give the boss bad news. The most reliable feedback is personal observation, especially spontaneous, unscheduled visits. It is not a matter of distrusting subordinates; it's a matter of distrusting communications. Failure to see for oneself is the primary reason for persisting on a course of action long after it has ceased to be effective. According to Peter Drucker, "One needs organized information for the feedback. One needs reports and figures. But unless one builds one's feedback around direct exposure to reality—unless one disciplines oneself to go out and look—one condemns oneself to a sterile dogmatism and with it, to ineffectiveness."

Authors Peters and Austin defined "management by walking around (MBWA)" as a common sense leadership formula, which ensures management's knowledge of workers, customers, and problems. MBWA keeps the senior leader in touch and permits him to listen to, empathize with, and praise the work force. Effective leaders get out of their offices and expect subordinate managers to do the same. Seeing is better than any computer printout, and it is not hearsay. MBWA leads to innovation and rapid problem solving because the existence of the problem is discovered sooner.

Seeing is better than any computer printout, and it is not hearsay.

MBWA is as valuable in the textile plant and modern university as in a military organization. The leader gets out of the office and gets the pulse of the organization. It has been my experience as a senior military commander and twice college/school president that seldom was there an instance when I visited the various commodity sections (motor transport, communications, supply or medical) or the dormitory and talked to the teachers and students that I didn't learn something that I should act upon. And as we are reminded in Benjamin Franklin's *Poor Richard's Almanac*, "The eye of the master will do more work than both his hands."

In summary, I support former U.S. Army General Melvin Zais' leadership formula, "Decide, Explain, and Enforce." If time is of the essence—omit the explanation and emphasize the enforcement. Without his supervision and oversight, the leader doesn't know where his explanation was inadequate and what needs reemphasis and reinforcement.

SECTION 34

DISCIPLINE AND SELF-DISCIPLINE

"Nothing emboldens sin so much as mercy."
William Shakespeare

"Self-discipline is that which, next to virtue, truly and
essentially raises one man above the other."
Joseph Addison

There exists organizational discipline and individual self-discipline. Organizational discipline exists when the senior leadership enforces the standards, policies, and procedures established for the organization. Self-discipline is learned in the home, school, or in an organization that demands a set of standards and is unwavering in their enforcement to the extent that the worker adopts the standards for himself. The military is an example. Often, career military personnel adapt to the early a.m. reveille until it becomes a lifetime habit. Conservative dress and hygiene often become lifetime habits. Military schools and colleges are good at instilling self-discipline, because there are real consequences for failure to measure up to established expectations.

According to psychologist John Rosemond, writing for the *Richmond Times-Dispatch,* discipline is compelling—not persuasive. Discipline is unequivocal; it's not about rules and legalism. It is about leadership, teaching, command, and communications. It involves compassion, firmness, and the appropriate use of consequences.

Whether in the unit or workplace, it requires order, synergy, and exactness. After my many years as a Marine officer, I can spend thirty minutes in a military unit, school, or company and tell something about the leader, his standards, and the discipline within the organization. Order and appearance are constants in disciplined organizations.

Order and appearance are constants in disciplined organizations.

Disciplined organizations are distinguished by accountability. People are held accountable for their work. The leader leaves no doubt who is responsible for which task and is resolute in expecting the task to be accomplished to standard and on time. If it is not completed to his liking, the responsible individual receives a private word of reproof minimally.

Undoubtedly, one of the most difficult challenges facing the leader is where to draw the line on discipline. Military discipline is exacting and enforced by more severe consequences. In the civilian workplace, one generally finds a more relaxed environment where some freedom exists particularly in personal appearance and dress. I have always been disappointed in the example set by professional athletes and the tolerance exhibited by the ownership of professional teams. Professional basketball players with bodies decorated with numerous tattoos, colored hair, and unshaven appearance say something about the standards set by the ownership. In contrast, the late owner of the New York Yankees, George Steinbrenner, showed his insistence on higher standards when he directed future Hall of Fame pitcher Randy Johnson to cut his locks when he joined the Yankees.

I have always been taken by the wisdom and thinking of the great sailor, John Paul Jones. His treatise on accountability, discipline, and the manner of a leader is timeless:

> It is by no means enough that an officer of the Navy should be a capable mariner. He must be that, of course, but also a great deal more. He should be, as well, a gentleman of liberal education, refined manner, punctilious courtesy, and the nicest sense of honor. He should not only be able to express himself clearly and with force in his own language

both with tongue and pen, but he should be versed in French and Spanish.

He should be the soul of tact, patience, justice, firmness and charity. No meritorious act of a subordinate should escape his attention or be let pass without its reward, if even the reward be only one word of approval. Conversely, he should not be blind to a single fault in any subordinate, though at the same time he should be quick and unfailing to distinguish error from malice, thoughtlessness from incompetency, and well-meant shortcoming from heedless or stupid blunder. As he should be universal and impartial in his rewards and approval of merit, so should he be judicial and unbending in his punishment or reproof of misconduct.[15]

The senior executive in any organization sets and enforces the standards of his unit, business, school, or other entity. The good ones will walk point on discipline and the organization will benefit in significant ways. Of course, there can be overzealous discipline where the methods can create morale issues that are insurmountable for the leader. In this case, solutions are few and intervention is often necessary from above.

---

15   Jones, John Paul. "Inspirational Journies," www.goodreads.com

SECTION 35

BALANCED EXCELLENCE

"In the race for quality (excellence), there is no finish line."
David Kearns, former CEO of Xerox.

Balanced excellence is a concept for success. I first heard of it from U.S. Marine Colonel Hank Stackpole (later to rise to the rank of Lieutenant General). According to then Colonel Stackpole, the winner strives to excel across the spectrum of his span of control. Likewise, a battalion commander I worked for in Vietnam used to preach that, "If we took care of the little things, the big things would take care of themselves." His theory seemed to bear fruit for as he berated us about things that were perceived as trivial to the officers of the battalion, the battalion performed superbly in the field, accumulating amazing statistics in weapons and prisoners of war captured, and enemy killed in action while maintaining a relatively low friendly casualty rate.

A *balanced excellence* approach to one's duties, if applied conscientiously, will result in recognition in areas never conceived beforehand. The seasoned leader strives for first place in every endeavor. He, therefore, receives much affirmation, is soon widely respected, and his pursuit of excellence across the spectrum of his responsibilities leads him to positions of greater responsibility and, hence, greater recognition. It doesn't take a mathematics wizard to see the exponential gains in recognition and respect acquired from a balanced excellence mindset, one that attacks mediocrity head on, from the flank, and from the rear.

SECTION 36

COMPLACENCY – PLATEAUING – PLUNGING

"Never mistake motion for action."
Ernest Hemingway

Success can breed failure in any organization as it is the garden for complacency. Complacency, subsequent to success, results in plateauing. According to Robert Kriegel and Louis Patler in their book, *If It Ain't Broke ... Break It*, "Plateauing occurs when the individual or the organization stops growing and moving upward. In fact, experience shows that plunging quickly follows plateauing." We have all seen this in the workplace as well as on the athletic field. When senior leaders begin to feel comfortable with their performance or the performance of their unit, the warning light comes on. Experience and instinct tell them that when all seems to be running well, when their comfort level begins to peg, it is time to get out of the office and exercise their curiosity. Invariably, something has gone awry, and by talking to the rank and file, they can head off the problem before plateauing turns to plunging.

According to author Robert Townsend, managers tend to make their biggest mistakes in things they've previously done best. In business, as elsewhere, hubris is the unforgivable sin of arrogance born of success. As the Greeks put it, "hubris is followed inexorably and inevitably by nemesis."

Personal experiences as a commander in the U.S. Marine Corps taught me that whenever I came to believe that my unit was at the summit in terms of performance, something serious was already occurring in the bowels of the organization that would soon upset my euphoria. In time, I became a bit of a pessimist, and whenever my ego began to pique, I quickly began to personally investigate by talking to folks two levels down in the unit. Usually, I could find some festering problem whether it was a racial misunderstanding, a leadership issue in a subordinate unit, or a morale or employee integrity problem that had not reached my level. Of course, discovering the problem early simplifies its resolution.

Some have written recently that pessimists tend to be effective leaders. In my judgment, there is truth in the theory. It might be better stated that experience enhances one's ability to lead effectively, because it nurtures ever-present doubt and causes one to constantly *what if* the environment for potential problems and plateauing or plunging performance.

SECTION 37

TITHE TO LEARNING

"Originality is nothing but judicious imitation."
Voltaire (Francois Marie Aroulet)

"It's but little good you'll do watering the last year's crops."
George Eliot (Marian Evans Cross)

"If you think education is expensive—try ignorance."
Derek Bok

*"There is always one more thing you can do to influence the
situation in your favor."*
LTG Hal Moore

Some years ago while attending a course on crisis action planning, I heard retired U.S. Army Lieutenant General Sam Wilson speak. General Wilson later became the President of Hampden-Sydney College in Farmville, Virginia. He is well known as one of the infamous Merrill's Marauders of World War II fame, a former Deputy Director of the Central Intelligence Agency, and once the Director of the Defense Intelligence Agency. He admonished us "to devote 10 percent of our time to learning, be it formal professional education, individual study, or just plain reading."

When authors and leadership research partners, Bennis and Nanus, asked their research subjects about the personal qualities necessary for success, little was said regarding charisma, dress, intellect, or time management. More than any other qualities, they said that successful managers are perpetual learners. In today's changing environment, those who are not continually stretching, growing, and striving for understanding do not survive.

> **In today's changing environment, those who are not continually stretching, growing, and striving for understanding do not survive.**

Some would conclude that television and the web have supplanted books as the primary attitude developer or attitude changer in America. This is probably the case in the lives of too many Americans who have completed their formal education. It is hard to argue the role that television plays in the perception of current events in this country, but one has to stretch the truth to categorize television as a prominent educational tool in the American home. As American author and critic, Marya Mannes wrote, "A person can be fascinated by movies and diverted by television, but they are a series of snacks. Books are the real nourishment of the human mind." Even books have changed, and they can be found online or in electronic book form. Nonetheless, hard copy or electronic, they remain the primary purveyor of wisdom (See Section 4).

To be successful in today's world, one must be current. The best way to stay current is through study and reading. One need not read from only the writings of those in his or her profession. In fact, the contrary is true. Leaders and managers in the private and public sectors can learn from the writings of the late leadership and management experts General George Patton, Admiral Hyman Rickover, as well as management gurus Peter Drucker, and Harold Geneen of ITT fame. Military leaders can learn from the likes of Mark McCormick, Norman Vincent Peale, and Harvey Mackay. All can learn from the master of human skills as portrayed so well by Donald T. Phillips in his *Lincoln on Leadership*.

The art of leading is not something that is accomplished in a week-long seminar or weekly one-hour training sessions. Leadership training involves continuous instruction, practical on-the-job experience, and years of self-study of books and periodicals on the techniques and philosophies of proven leaders. It is well known that leaders are not born, but made. Although appearance, intelligence, and charisma make it easier for some to lead than others, all learn to lead if they are willing to pay the price in terms of education and training.

Leadership training involves continuous instruction, practical on-the-job experience, and years of self-study of books and periodicals on the techniques and philosophies of proven leaders.

Those who are well read and educated in their profession and the art of leadership seem to be more confident in their environment and innovative in their approach to their jobs. They appear to be less imprisoned by the paradigms of the profession and their particular position than the less informed. Education seems to filter new information through the paradigm making it less fearsome. The world is full of "copycat thinkers." Senior leaders and managers display confidence, originality, new approaches, and new ideas through the study of their profession. "Tell me what you read," observed Goethe, "and I will tell you what you are."

THE SCHOOL AND ITS CUSTOMER

*"Service is just a day-in, day-out, ongoing, never-ending,
unremitting, persevering, compassionate type of activity."*
Leon Gorman

"Manhood, not scholarship, is the first aim of education."
E. T. Seton

If there is anything I have taken from W. Edwards Deming's *Total Quality Management* (TQM), it is that many organizations do not know the identity of their customer. As a former secondary public school teacher, vice president of a fine liberal arts college, president of a military two-year college, and president of a military college preparatory school, I quickly recognize schools that put their students first—schools that genuinely care about the character and academic success of *all* of their students. As a general rule, private institutions walk the extra mile to ensure student learning and parental feedback. Private schools realize that the student and his parents are their customers.

Generally, students are treated with care; parents receive timely and frequent written and oral feedback; and the administration and faculty see to those things that ensure the student wants to return each year. Why? Because the students are their *customers* and *the school's economic engine,* and they know it. I realize that *customer* is not a coveted term among educators because of its business or economic connotation, and I do not care if one substitutes *client* for *customer.* But the truth is that the student is the one served by our schools. His development is the school's mission and the reason for its existence.

Because the students are their customers and the school's economic engine and they know it.

I have observed public schools where the faculty acted as if the student were fortunate to be there, and it was the student's responsibility to come in motivated to learn. Teachers provide the material, and if the students does not care to receive it, so be it. This is not to criticize public schools, because I believe in public schools, and I realize that the public schools have many extraordinary teachers. I only draw on the comparison of public versus private because of the necessity for private schools to see the student and his parents as their customers.

I have also observed some professors at fine colleges whose primary focus was on their "A" students. They would adopt the young intellectual, use him in research projects, and boast of his abilities publicly. However, I am more interested in the average and below average student. Most professors can teach the bright and focused young person from the stable home who is motivated for college. His parents may be college graduates and prominent in the community. But, I am drawn to the professors who thrive on the leadership challenge of motivating and teaching the unkempt, not-so-bright student who comes to college disinterested, distracted, moody, and sometimes disruptive. Some of these students are athletes and are in college simply to *play ball*. They should be viewed by faculty members as opportunities to turn on the light of education.

Somehow, we have to make school something that young people anticipate with enthusiasm. The atmosphere has to be that the student is special; that he is the object of our attention; and that the rules are there to make school a positive experience for him. Great effort must be exerted to ensure he knows that the entire faculty is there to help him and genuinely cares whether he succeeds. This is not to say that the administration must be tolerant of inappropriate behavior. Indeed, inappropriate behavior must be addressed by firm and consistent sanctions to include suspension or dismissal from school when necessary. Sometimes when sanctions or punishments are levied "administrators are not doing it to them—but for them."

Sometimes when sanctions or punishments are levied "administrators are not doing it to them—but for them."

This is but one example of an organization that has not always determined its customer. The caring principal or college administrator who has bathed himself in student and parent feedback and cares equally about all of his students will see them reap the benefits scholastically, academically, and in the resultant achievement tests.

It is not surprising that so many leaders are great teachers, because that is what leadership is all about—shaping attitudes and helping others perform at or near their God-given abilities.

SECTION 39

HIP-SHOOTERS AND FOOT DRAGGERS

"Life is the art of drawing sufficient conclusions from insufficient premises."
Samuel Butler

*"Soon after a hard decision,
something inevitably occurs to cast doubt.
Holding steady against that doubt usually proves the
decision."*
R. I. Fitzhenry

*"Decide promptly, but never give any reasons.
Your decisions may be right,
but your reasons are sure to be wrong."*
Lord William Murray Mansfield

*"Never explain.
Your friends do not need it and your enemies will not
believe it anyway."*
Elbert Hubbard

Effective decision-making is the sword of the senior leader. He is trained to assimilate large amounts of data, organize it mentally, quickly cost-benefit it, and make a rational decision. Additionally, he can take small amounts of data, quickly assess it, cost-benefit it, and make a *timely* rational decision. In reality, most decisions are of the latter type. Hence, this leader makes critical and timely decisions under pressure in the heat of the moment and often in the absence of relevant information. Those decisions are usually the ones that carry the day.

The senior leader realizes that, most of the time, not all of the desired data is available to facilitate the right decision. However, he has learned to *trust his instincts*. He senses when sufficient data is present and when to step back and ask more questions. Robert Ringer's *The Natural Law of Balance* says, "The universe is in balance ... you should never delude yourself about the reality that you must always give up something in order to gain something. If you can't see one or more offsets when making a decision, you'd best call time-out and study the situation more carefully, because it probably means that you're overlooking more important facts."

What can be more frustrating than to work for a leader or manager who lacks the confidence to make timely decisions? He is the same procrastinator who won't act until every element of data is in. He relishes ad-hoc committees, focus groups, and study groups, as they are his way of delay and disguise his lack of courage and confidence. He invariably employs consensus decision-making, which may only maintain the status quo and can be a play-it-safe methodology, which, if overused, can guarantee mediocrity.

> **He relishes ad-hoc committees, focus groups, and study groups, as they are his way of delay and disguise his lack of courage and confidence.**

My intent is not to criticize the thorough, deliberate, and organized decision-maker who refuses to act when more and better information is available, and the staff has failed to provide it. Furthermore, I realize that the world is also full of impulsive, hip-shooters who act with little or no information and are the antithesis of the successful leader. I simply want to shock the procrastinator into action and help him realize that leaders must routinely make decisions with insufficient data. The acceptance of risk is the natural order of the day for leaders. Failure to act in a timely manner is tantamount to defeat in business, the public sector, politics, war, and athletics.

Failure to act in a timely manner is tantamount to defeat in business, the public sector, politics, war, and athletics.

The environment has much to do with the leader's willingness to accept risk. His perception of how he is viewed by the organizational hierarchy, the media, the public, his subordinates, and even his peers, impacts his willingness to trust his instincts and be decisive. For example, when General Meade assumed command of the Army of the Potomac in June 1863, General Lee knew that Meade would be cautious until he was more comfortable in his new position. By contrast General Lee was confident in his position; hence, he assumed great risk in attacking Meade's Army over open terrain, resulting in his resounding defeat at Gettysburg. In this case, Lee trusted his own instincts notwithstanding advice to the contrary from Major General Longstreet and others.

The best leaders recognize that a decision is only as good as the information on which it is based. They know how to get the facts by asking the right questions that drive straight to the heart of the matter. They sense when a subordinate is hedging or avoiding the hard question, either because he does not know the answer or because the answer is unpleasant. It doesn't take an experienced leader long to plot the reliability and dependability of the members of his staff. He knows who to query thoroughly and who to accept at face value. According to Euripides (485 – 406 BC), "A man's most valuable trait is a judicious sense of what not to believe."

The prudent leader will not routinely make his decisions based on input from only one level down. He gets to know people two levels down and often gets first-hand facts from the rank and file. He realizes that the lower he goes for information, the less tainted it becomes. The mere fact that he goes down two or more levels for his information does much to keep staff members on their toes. It does wonders for the morale and attitude of the junior leadership and rank and file to know that their opinions count, especially when their comments are clearly portrayed in the final decision.

Organizational hierarchy is in itself inimical to efficient decision-making. As decision or issue papers work their way up the chain of command with review and recommendation attached at every level; time and money are lost. The leader realizes this and empowers his subordinate leaders and managers to make decisions at the lowest level possible.

Organizational hierarchy is in itself inimical to efficient decision-making.

The one type of decision that always requires patience and forethought is a decision concerning firing, transferring, or promoting personnel. Through the years, I have observed many leaders in organizations routinely shuffle the deck by moving people in various forms of reorganization, and I have come to the conclusion that the turbulence and loss of continuity in such madness undercuts productivity. Effective executives contemplate personnel decisions carefully and act only when reasonably certain that the turbulence and loss of continuity associated with the move will pay dividends in the long run and stop the bleeding in the short term. Such decisions may drive the need for *rapid* decisions to redress situations that threaten operations *now*. These leaders are cognizant of the value, need, and costs inherent in *shaking up* the organization and weigh the competing courses of action carefully before executing personnel decisions.

SECTION 40

DELEGATION OR EMPOWERMENT

"Delegate but don't abdicate."
Anonymous

"There is a difference between being in control and controlling."
Anonymous

Effective senior leadership includes the responsibility of preparing others to assume greater responsibility and delegating the authority to make decisions consistent with that responsibility. Nevertheless, egos tend to get in the way, and many are never able to adequately delegate sufficient authority to maximize the potential of the organization. The best leaders find gratification in developing, directing, and observing subordinates assume responsibility and achieve success on their own.

> **The best leaders find gratification in developing, directing, and observing subordinates assume responsibility and achieve success on their own.**

The criteria for delegation seem to be more intuitive than intellectual. The following maxims seem to prevail:

- Trust and confidence in subordinates comes first.

- Risk correlates with the amount of authority delegated.

- The greater the organizational complexity—the greater the need for delegation.

- Less delegation occurs during crisis management.

I have always had more confidence in the written word than the spoken word. It probably dates back to my time as a platoon and company commander in Vietnam where misunderstanding of orders could be deadly. Since then, I have concluded that some people simply do not take verbal direction as official, or at least, as serious as written direction. It has been written that the nerves leading from the eye to the brain are many times more sensitive than those leading from the ear to the brain. So, if one expects strict compliance with directions, reduce them to writing—clear, concise, and explicit.

> **Some people simply do not take verbal direction as official, or at least, as serious as written direction.**

With the above as a backdrop, delegation is a key ingredient to winning. It has become increasingly difficult for leaders and managers in most organizations to juggle all the balls simultaneously. If it were possible, it wouldn't be necessary to have assistants, deputies, and staff.

Contemporary management theory and many academicians proclaim delegation as empowerment. Whatever we name it, the higher one ascends the hierarchy of leadership, the more one needs to throttle back, lower the volume, listen better, and delegate responsibility. Similarly, it is important to loosen the reins and permit others to think, lead, and manage. The results will speak for themselves.

I have probably offended portions of the academic community frequently by referring to the hierarchy of leadership. I am aware that some in the academic community and many leaders of the academic professional organizations advocate flat organizations devoid of all or most of the hierarchy existent in traditional organizations. Some have written that flat is the future of corporate America, and if corporations want to survive, they must adapt accordingly. I concur that we can strip some of the hierarchal layers out and should (for economic and timely decision-making reasons), but the hierarchy will remain, even if it doesn't show up on the organizational diagram. Somebody is still in charge; someone else is number two; some are supervising the work of others; some are approving and disapproving policies, and so forth. At least, it better be that way or the hard decisions will be compromises. The very nature of compromising in order to appease the opinions of others leads to sub-optimization, which in time can put the organization in the boneyard.

The very nature of compromising in order to appease the opinions of others leads to sub-optimization, which in time can put the organization in the boneyard.

Much has been written about the necessity for *participative management*. Author Max DePree is the former CEO and Chairman of the Board for Herman Miller, one of the most successful and productive furniture companies in America. According to Max, participative management is not democratic nor do employees have a vote. What they do have is a say relative to important business decisions. In other words, the staff is consulted, but the decision remains with the boss. This is a philosophy I learned in the Marines. The leader is accountable and makes decisions based on the best information available. I would add that staff members must first earn my trust and confidence; they must establish their credibility.

I recently read in an academic journal that, "Collaboration is the key to the future of education." Collaboration is a euphemism for "working together." I agree that working together effectively is important, and it is the leader's responsibility to create that synergy, but collaboration is not a new phenomenon that is the *be all, and end all* for education or anything else. In fact, too much collaboration can lead to stagnation, unnecessary appeasement, and less than productive compromise on what really needs to get done.

But collaboration is not a new phenomenon that is the be all, and end all for education or anything else.

Senior leaders walk point when they possess the executive courage to weigh their options and decide the matter whether it involves personnel, procurement, expansion, reorganization, capital expenditures, or any other decision that carries substantial risk. Walking point involves stepping into the unknown with poise and confidence knowing that right or wrong, the preparation is complete, the decision is made, and the naysayers and half-steppers best step aside.

Delegation, collaboration, and risk acceptance are all in the leader's kit bag but none so much as his vision, accountability, and will to succeed.

COMPROMISE, CONSENSUS, AND SUB–OPTIMIZATION

"Pick battles big enough to matter, small enough to win."
Jonathan Kozol

"When war does come, my advice is to draw the sword and throw away the scabbard."
General Stonewall Jackson

"It seems to be the law of the land, inflexible and inexorable, that those who will not risk cannot win."
Rear Admiral John Paul Jones

The prudent leader realizes that it is counterproductive to take on every issue vehemently even when they are sure their position is the correct one. We have all seen those who are always looking for a fight and will go to the mat on the slightest of issues. These are the ones who are referred to as obstinate, hard-headed, rigid, and too disruptive and contentious for positions of greater responsibility.

The effective leader first examines an issue to determine its long-term relevancy. He knows that sometimes it is better to intentionally give in on one or two lesser issues in order to put the organization in a better bargaining position for the real battle ahead.

The following guidelines are offered:

- Pick your battles carefully; there will be times to go to the mat, but they must be judiciously selected.

- In negotiations, compromise only when you can't win, and the compromise is better than the status quo.
- Show humility when you win.

Although compromise is occasionally warranted, it can be the bane of progress. "Sub-optimal" frequently describes the results. Organizations that routinely resort to compromise, especially to avoid controversy, can be short-lived. Seasoned leaders compromise when they cannot win, when the compromise is an improvement over the status quo, or when it provides useful leverage elsewhere. Compromise is also acceptable to buy time and better circumstances favoring optimization.

> **Seasoned leaders compromise when they cannot win, when the compromise is an improvement over the status quo, or when it provides useful leverage elsewhere.**

The best that one can expect is to win *most of the time* when one is right! Those who pick their battles indiscriminately weaken their credibility and dilute their influence on the real issues.

Seeking consensus on the significant issues within one's own staff for the sake of inclusion or appeasement is a form of compromise. The effective decision-maker listens to the wisdom and views of the staff and makes the right decision based on sound judgment and common sense. Feelings are rarely part and parcel to effective executive decision-making.

> **Feelings are rarely part and parcel to effective executive decision-making.**

SECTION 42

PICKING YOUR ENEMIES

"You saw his weakness, and he will never forgive you."
Johann Christoph Friedrich von Schiller

"A man cannot be too careful in the choice of his enemies."
Oscar Wilde

"Anyone can become angry—that is easy.
But to be angry with the right person,
to the right degree, at the right time,
for the right purpose, and in the right way—
that is not easy."
Aristotle

Prudent senior leaders never make an enemy unless it is time. They realize that whenever one intentionally makes an enemy, he unintentionally makes several others who will add their resistance to that of the "original" enemy. According to Harvey Mackay, "The clubhouse men of the world are just waiting for a chance to kick you in the ass. You may not be watching them, but they're watching you, (especially if you are successful—my emphasis) and the more arrogant you are, whether you're an eleven-year-old kid or some self-important business type, the better the odds they'll find a way to get even." Of course, there are times when it is necessary to make an enemy, but indiscriminate statements and actions that alienate others are wrought with consequences. And if there are nicks in one's armor, rest assured that every enemy will find them and exploit them.

One of the deadliest enemy makers in an organization is gossip. Additionally, it is one of the primary perpetrators of division within an organization. It is an enemy producer of the highest order. As the old saying goes, "bad talk always comes back." King Solomon was right in Proverbs 10:18, ". . . whoever spreads slander is a fool." Executive leaders must not participate in gossip or tolerate it!

One of the deadliest enemy makers in an organization is gossip.

The best executives use confrontation judiciously. Confrontation, especially public confrontation, causes friction within the organization. It often leads to the choosing of sides and can cause lasting resentment that is detrimental to the organization as a team. At times, confrontation is necessary; but the successful leader will employ it sparingly and privately when it becomes the only viable option. According to Attila the Hun, as translated by Wess Roberts in his priceless little book, *Leadership Secrets of Attila the Hun,* "Chieftains should never rush into confrontation."

While it is important not to make enemies external to the organization, it is also important to minimize enemies within the organization—yes, even if you are the boss. Again, I draw on the writings of Harvey Mackay. He writes that the leader should not be his own hatchet man. As the head of the organization, Mackay writes, "You have to get someone who can make the tough, mean, unpopular decisions and can take the fall when they get too tough, mean, and unpopular." I think there is wisdom to Mackay's position in some situations. However, I disagree that the senior leader should delegate every unpopular decision or every personnel termination. Surely, department heads should be strong enough to carry some of the load. Mackay, however, advises that if the senior leader of the organization chooses to be the so-called hatchet man, he had better possess the following:

- exceptional intelligence with the ability to ask tough questions from 8:00 a.m. until quitting time, whenever that is;

- fair-mindedness (you might call it the ability to hit with either a left jab or a right cross);

- maintenance of extremely high performance standards for himself;

- commitment to keep his guard up at all times;

- the ability to shed criticism like a duck shedding raindrops.

> **While it is important not to make enemies external to the organization, it is also important to minimize enemies within the organization—yes, even if you are the boss.**

Few of us have our act wound so tight that we can afford to continually be our own hatchet man, and none of us want the stress that comes with that role. I don't care for the term hatchet man and believe that the senior leader must personally execute the termination of all who report directly to him. Termination of others can and should be delegated to department heads depending on the nature and cause of the termination.

The late Bill Walsh, former head coach of the three-time Super Bowl Champion San Francisco 49ers, summarized it nicely:

> In building the organization, I also stressed the importance of not making enemies. We didn't want to expend energy on anything other than the project at hand. We couldn't afford an enemy, whether it was NFL coaches and management, league employees, players, the press, college coaches, and local citizens. One enemy could do more damage than the good done by a hundred friends.[16]

---

16 BILL WALSH. Building a Champion. (St. Martin's Press, New York) 1991.

SECTION 43

THE MATING DANCE

*"The fellow who says he'll meet you halfway usually thinks
he is standing on the dividing line."*
Orlando A. Battista

*"Deliberation is the work of many men.
Action, of one alone."*
Charles de Gaulle

While serving as the Chief, Plans and Force Development, J-5, U.S.
Southern Command (SOUTHCOM) in the mid-1980s, I led the
planning effort for seven military contingency war plans for Central
and South America. This planning occurred when communist
insurgencies were replete throughout the region. Nicaragua planning
was particularly contentious, and there were strong indicators that
we might have to deploy a very significant force to seize the beaches
and airfields and evacuate hundreds of U.S. citizens from many parts
of the country.

Sometimes it could take several years to complete a controversial
plan like the one for Nicaragua. The four services would fight like cats
over their role and the size of their force. There were many meetings,
and they were often classified Code Word, "Top Secret." I would
become agitated with the dissent and obstinate positions of the various
military service planners on the first day of each meeting. Clearly,
each service planner came with an agenda. Of course, all considered
themselves tacticians and had a better plan centered on their own
force capabilities. However, the Commander-in-Chief of the Southern
Command (CINCSOUTH) was a four-star General, and I had his

guidance before I led each meeting. After the first-day verbal firefight between the services and the realization that the General would budge very little on the concept of operations, planners would return on day two, and we would make significant progress. I recall Colonel Bill Comee's counsel: "Jim, the first day is always the 'mating dance.'"

Executive leaders should not set their expectations too high for the first day of any serious or protracted negotiation. They must realize that the first day is generally "the mating dance" where the "cahunas" spar; by the second day, things begin to break.

> **Executive leaders must realize that the first day is generally "the mating dance" where the "cahunas" spar; by the second day, things begin to break.**

Although the example above applies to military planning and how the military services often compete to be the centerpiece of any operation, the principle applies to negotiations in "buy-outs," sales, and other deliberations where there will be winners and losers or at least, one party will come out better off than others.

SECTION 44

COMMUNICATIONS

"Communications dominate war; broadly considered,
they are the most important single element in strategy,
political or military."
Alfred T. Mahan

Benjamin Disraeli wrote that, "One writes not simply to be understood but not to be misunderstood." We have all written something that made perfect sense to us, and yet it was completely misconstrued by the reader, to our dismay. I recall the colossal breakdown in corporate communications when General Motors attempted to market the Chevy Nova in Latin America, not realizing that "no va" meant "it won't go" in Spanish.

I suggest that there is no profession more dependent on clear communications than the military. Military operations must be clearly understood by every subordinate element, because clarity can determine victory or defeat and life or death. Some are still debating Jeb Stuart's misunderstanding of Robert E. Lee's orders at Cavalry Field at Gettysburg, which may have cost Lee the battle and the South the war.

Of course, NASA and other scientists must write effectively, and doctors must write clinically. While there is no endeavor that benefits from poor writing, I am convinced that the legal profession never heard of Disraeli. One should see the language in some of the lawyer-produced contracts that I have to try to understand.

Over time, I have learned that I don't have to sign confusing, ambiguous contracts. It is my responsibility to ensure I know exactly what I am agreeing to or obligating my organization to. So I do not hesitate to rewrite lawyer-prepared contracts that are esoteric and impossible for many to understand.

DR. JAMES H. BENSON

Over time, I have learned that I don't have to sign confusing, ambiguous contracts.

In any complex or sizeable venture, writing skills—brevity and clarity—are critical, and knowing and understanding the audience is close behind. Writing is our thinking made visible. Most write better than they speak, since they have longer to construct their passages. As earlier stated, I have greater confidence in the written word than the spoken word. Senior leaders who reduce their vision, planning guidance, and taskings to writing are prudent and lessen the risk of misunderstanding.

Yes, being able to write coherent instructions and intent is important. But it is also important to be able to deliver them orally at times when emphasis and inflection are important. It is hard to motivate your team with a policy paper when action by the recipient is one's intent.

I am tired of politicians who pontificate on the need for "ideas." I hear candidates rant about their own ideas and the absence of ideas by their opponent. I care little about candidate ideas that rarely come to fruition. I am interested in their previous record of action and change. We have become a nation that elects candidates based on ideas, oratory, and debating skills—whatever happened to character, leadership, and the *ability to get things done*?

I am tired of politicians who pontificate on the need for "ideas."

Good, bad, or indifferent, communications skills are the critical component of executive leadership. Poor communications skills can create enormous problems for the senior leader while strong communications skills can be the difference between success and failure.

Communications skills are the critical component of executive leadership.

204

SECTION 45

PROBLEM PRESENTERS

"A problem clearly stated is a problem half solved."
Dorothea Brande

*"Focus 90% of your time on solutions and only 10% of your
time on problems."*
Anthony J. D'Angelo

"The first responsibility of a leader is to define reality."
Max De Pree

Executives do not suffer staff members for long who continually present problems and issues without simultaneously bringing alternatives and a recommended course of action to solve the problem or issue. Problems are best solved at the lowest level possible, because the impact and understanding of the problem is stronger there. Leaders who shoot from the hip and personally tackle each problem with minimal input from others will suffer much from their exuberance. The staff will gladly surrender the problem and the responsibility for its *solution*. The best executive leaders resist the temptation to immediately respond to an identified problem; they wait for the courses of action and pros and cons of each.

Leaders must require proposed solutions to activate the thinking of the staff. Moreover, when problems are presented with potential solutions by staff, they are forced to define the problem more analytically. Try this and you will be surprised how often your decision differs from your initial reaction when you were originally presented with the problem or issue.

SECTION 46

OUR MORTAL ENEMY

"The only difference between man and men all over the world is one of degree, and not of kind, even as there is between trees of the same species. Where is the cause for anger, envy, or discrimination?"
Mahatma Gandhi

I grew up in a southwest Virginia family that privately expressed racial prejudice towards the *negroes*. It wasn't hatred they expressed, but even my devoutly Christian grandmother believed that the *white* and *negro* races were unequal. I recall when the *black* families began to move into our pristine middle-class neighborhood, like other *whites*, we moved. I had every reason to adopt their prejudiced beliefs. But for some reason, I did not buy into inequality in perception or opportunity, even then. I was very curious about the black families. My favorite baseball player was Willie Mays, and I admired him as a man and as a great centerfielder. Additionally, although not vocal, I had great sympathy for the blacks during the race riots of the 60s. Even then, I had experienced virtually no interaction with them, as we went to separate schools.

Later when I was teaching and coaching post-college, there were no black students in our schools. It was not until U.S. Marine Corps Officer Candidate School in1968 that I interacted with blacks, and the first was my drill instructor whom I quickly came to fear, admire, and respect. Within a year I was in command of a platoon in Vietnam, which was approximately 20 percent black Marines. It was while in the rice patties, mountains, and jungles of Vietnam that I realized how wrong our country had been for so many years. In combat, race, culture, and former prejudices take a backseat to mutual respect, manhood, and survival. Whether officer, enlisted, race, or religion—little mattered except duty, survival, and a genuine caring for one another. To this day, I marvel at how in Vietnam our unit (squads, platoons, and company) worked together. A mix of whites, Mexicans, American Indians, and blacks—we fought, laughed, commiserated, and occasionally imbibed. Some of them, I will never forget. After all, we were in hell together.

There was a black lance corporal by the name of King (not sure I ever knew his first name) who survived his year in the "bush" with two Purple Hearts as I recall. He mostly kept to himself, read the Bible, carried a couple of heavy duty law books in his pack and was often alone reading; he said he was going to be a lawyer, and I am sure he is today. King was our self-appointed lay preacher and led our Sunday morning prayer meetings in the bush. When I arrived, King had already spent too much time *walking point*—very hazardous duty in the Nam. I insisted that King not walk point any longer as he was on the very backside of his tour, and I didn't want to lose him. However, the troops had so much confidence in him, and he would insist on walking point on the most dangerous missions. LCPL King survived the war and was one of many black Marines who are memorable to me.

It was not long before my sympathy turned to respect and admiration of blacks. I concluded that given the opportunity, not only were they equal to whites intellectually, but they were generally, superior athletically. I also marveled at their rhythm and musical talent, oratory skills, passion for life, and leadership. In a very short period of time and with greater opportunity, blacks have achieved great things in America—not the least of which is the achievement of the presidency of our great nation. Thus, I disdain the term *racial tolerance*, because it implies we must *put up* with one another. I prefer the term *racial* or *cultural appreciation*, because it is a better description of what we must feel or learn to feel. I have zero patience for racial slurs as my staff and cadets have learned at the two military academies that I led. There is no room in America for a racial divide or intolerance. Racism is a mortal enemy of America, and senior leaders must take a strong and vocal position relative to racial relations within their organizations.

Race remains a leadership challenge for senior leaders. Minority workers must know that you are color-blind when it comes to race. For them to know this, they have to see it—not just hear it from you.

They see in the racial climate the leader creates, especially his attitude and reaction to racial jokes, tolerance of racial comments, and equality in promotions.

Racism is a mortal enemy of America, and senior leaders must take a strong and vocal position relative to racial relations within their organizations.

SECTION 47

RECIPROCITY IN HUMAN INTERACTION

"A generous man will prosper; he who refreshes others will himself be refreshed."
Proverbs 12:25

The best leaders I have known have graduated from selfness to otherness. They possess an inherent character, which is giving in nature. Somehow, they have acquired an understanding that one reaps what one sows. Organizations revolve around personal relationships. These relationships are created in a myriad of ways. The magic about genuine, unselfish behavior demonstrated by leaders is that it is reciprocated. Solomon confirmed the principle of reciprocity in Proverbs 12:25 when he said, "A generous man will prosper; he who refreshes others will himself be refreshed." Ralph Waldo Emerson reinforced the principle; "It is one of the most beautiful compensations of this life that no man can sincerely try to help another without helping himself."

In spite of the evidence confirming these principles of successful leading and living, one of the toughest challenges in this life is to speak highly of, let alone assist one's contemporaries and competitors. Neither will *respected* senior leaders denigrate nor criticize contemporaries or competitors for personal or organizational gain.

According to the author, Robert Townsend, "Every success I've ever had came about because I was trying to help other people. Every promotion I got at American Express came about when I was up to my ears helping my associates be as effective as possible.... On the other hand, every time I had a really clever idea for making me a lot of money or for getting me into some interesting position, it turned out to be an utter failure."

The best leaders develop a habit of helping others unselfishly. It can be a struggle, and one has to work at it continually until it becomes habitual. If you want to be a successful and prosperous leader, try this:

- Do something for somebody in the organization daily.

- Never pass up an opportunity to help another or speak highly of another, and do so for contemporaries as well as competitors.

Try it for a week; you'll be amazed how others treat you and speak of your organization.

> **Never pass up an opportunity to help another or speak highly of another, and do so for contemporaries as well as competitors.**

SECTION 48

LONELINESS OR SOLITUDE

*"Conversation enriches the understanding, but solitude is
the school of genius."*
Edward Gibbon

*"There are times like the early morning hours when I prefer
my own company."*
Jim Benson

"Be still and know that I am God."
Psalm 46:10

Protestant theologian and professor, Paul Tillich may have captured the dilemma between loneliness and solitude when he wrote, "Language has created the word loneliness to express the pain of being alone and the word solitude to express the glory of being alone." There is little doubt that loneliness is accompanied by many maladies, but it is more debilitating to some than others. Everyone needs companionship, but the frequency and intensity varies from one person to another. Myers-Briggs accurately confirmed me as an introvert at heart (though my college friends would vehemently refute that statement), and my adult years have proven the fact. It is true that I often prefer my own company. Of course, I have learned to function in an extrovert's world but often wonder when they ever have time to think and contemplate.

The higher one climbs the ladder of responsibility, the more one must create and protect *thinking time*. Without it, there is no opportunity to envision, analyze, and create necessary change. The result can be that the leader and the organization get into a *stasis rut*, and the competition gains momentum or new competition moves into the market with a better message and product.

The higher one climbs the ladder of responsibility, the more one must create and protect thinking time.

My study or library is my fortress. I require before-dawn solitude holed up in my fortress away from the distractions and noise of the family. If one believes that he can stay up until 11:00 or 12:00 p.m. watching television, surfing the internet, or frequenting social media, he better keep his eye on his position longevity and balance sheet. Rising at 7:00 a.m. to be at work at 8 a.m. leaves no time to prepare for the work, no time to do your homework, or tend to one's spiritual devotions.

Someone once wrote that leaders must learn to be separate from the staff and workforce without really being distant. It is true that the senior leader must create some space between himself and those he leads. We have all heard the phrase that *familiarity breeds contempt.* This is why leading can be a lonely business.

Someone once wrote that leaders must learn to be separate from the staff and workforce without really being distant.

Of course, books are the refuge of the introvert. They are the defensible opportunity to go inside oneself and enjoy a reality other than the here and now. It is hard for an introvert and an extrovert to co-exist. My Mary is the extrovert in our marriage. She wants to talk while we read the newspaper, discuss the movie while we watch it, and express her every thought during the most important portion of the news. It can be exasperating, but she is a wonderful companion. How do you figure?

Books are the refuge of the introvert.

SECTION 49

TRUST YOUR INSTINCTS

"Instinct is untaught ability."
Alexander Bain

"Instinct is the nose of the mind."
Madame de Girardin

*"If necessity is the mother of invention, intuition is the
mother of vision."*
James Kouzes and Barry Posner

"Superb leadership is often a matter of superb instinct."
Colin Powell

Many of us doubt our precognitive abilities. I cannot estimate the number of times I have left the house and felt I had forgotten something only to discover thirty minutes later that I had. I've finally learned to trust my extrasensory memory. Now when I sense something is amiss, I stop, think, and look. One's extrasensory abilities are continually sending mental signals concerning decision making, safety, and recall. We literally have to train ourselves to trust these sensings. Many times it comes in the form of a hunch, something we are not trained to appreciate.

> **One's extrasensory abilities are continually sending mental signals concerning decision making, safety, and recall.**

Entrepreneurs are best at pursuing their hunches, although the successful ones probably do not refer to them as hunches. Professional judgment, intuition, gut feeling, instinct, and inner voice are applicable descriptors. Whatever they are called, I suspect entrepreneurs use them as take-off points for cost-benefit analysis and subsequent decisions to move forward.

Many never learn to trust their intuitive right brain. They are reluctant to place their success or failure at the feet of a strong sensing. Likewise, they do not want to be viewed as a "loose cannon." If they should fail, they want plenty of data that they thoroughly researched the issue before they ventured a decision. Unfortunately, many have become C.Y.A. managers and leaders.

Gerald Jackson in his book titled, *Executive ESP* wrote of our failure to trust our intuitive abilities.

> One such obstacle is over-reliance on the rational mind. Remember the Edsel? The Ford Motor Company has never lived down that design disaster back in the 50s. It remains the symbol of logical thinking unaided by inspiration. What research was done, what studies made? As a gesture toward the intuitive side of the brain, the company actually hired a poet, Marianne Moore, to come up with a name for the car. But in the end, the company ignored her suggestions ....[17]

Ralph Larsen, former chair and CEO of Johnson & Johnson, claims that failure to listen to his instincts resulted in some bad decisions. He explains that eleven years at Johnson & Johnson taught him the importance of trusting his intuition. According to Larsen, senior management deals with issues too complex and ambiguous for quantitative decision making. It is times like these when the intuitive senior leader with the knowledge and intuitive skills earns his big salary.

Experienced senior leaders trust their instincts. Alden Hayaski, writing for the *Harvard Business Review*, tells us that, "They hear the quiet alarms sounded by their intuitive brain. They investigate and

---

17   Gerald Jackson. *Executive ESP*. (Simon & Schuster, New York) 1990.

act on the possibilities presented by these instincts. They are alert for signals of opportunities waiting to be seized."

Successful executives trust their instincts and recognize them as a unique combination of knowledge, creativity, and experience. They may confront and disagree, but nonetheless, they will always confront and disagree while using judgment and forethought. Realizing that on occasion they will be wrong, they know that others will forgive errors in judgment but not ill motive. There are times when leaders must assume the point position; put the opposition opinions aside and decide, act, and not look back.

Successful executives trust their instincts and recognize them as a unique combination of knowledge, creativity, and experience.

SECTION 50

THOUGHTS ON EFFICIENCY

"I've learned that you shouldn't have a $1,000 meeting to solve a $100 problem."
H. J. Brown

"A person who has not done one-half his day's work by ten o'clock, runs a chance of leaving the other half undone."
Emily Brontë

The academics will harangue me unmercifully for addressing a subject so broad in such a short section. And, of course, efficiency and effectiveness are too broad to adequately cover without significant documentation, but I am going to touch on a few areas that have caused me heartburn in my years.

Once, in a prospering fitness center, I saw a poster that said, "Happy Hour starts at 5:00 a.m.!" This particular center opened its doors at 5:00 a.m., and the owner understood the importance of not only getting an early start himself, but also of catering to his customers who shared his *get things done* mentality.

Years ago when others would ask my opinion of the previous night's Jay Leno show, I would wonder how they thought they could be at the top of their game the following day without the rest their bodies and minds require. The fact is, most aren't ready to face the next day. They sleep a little later, go to the office, and immediately must field the telephone calls and electronic mail without any time to organize their day. Hence, they are continually in the catch-up mode, stressed out to the maximum, and finally go home distressed and remark how much they dislike their job.

There is no substitute for a 5:00 a.m. happy hour filled with devotions, exercise, solitude, morning coffee, and a day organized before the first call is ever taken.

So much has been written about the conduct and organization of meetings. I don't even like to talk about meetings except to say that too many are inconsistent with efficient operations. A requirement for meetings clearly exists, but in too many organizations the business day revolves around one meeting after another. When this is the case, efficiency takes a dive. Meetings invariably take too long, particularly when chaired by the boss who is an extrovert at heart and loves to hear himself pontificate. Some of my most frustrating meetings were at the behest of colonels with strong egos, eager to share *war stories*, neither of which were part of the meeting's purpose. In fact, many of the meetings were designated "staff coordination." Generally, a staff coordination meeting exists so that divisions and departments are heading in the same direction and on the same timeline. But this can usually be accomplished weekly in a short update, which is chaired and clocked by one sympathetic to the time constraints of the staff.

Many leaders use meetings to pass out verbal taskers to the staff, and, quite frankly, this works well for some. However, I am a firm believer in written taskers that provide some background, the task at hand, and the due date. This method risks administrative growth; but it gives the action officer a record of exactly what is required and when. It is time sensitive, because it can be delivered without waiting for the next meeting. With the advent of electronic mail, many are using written taskers but others still insist on the spoken word. The spoken word is exemplary of inefficiency in itself. It is subject to misinterpretation, poor hearing, and it cannot be reread for clarity.

> **The spoken word is exemplary of inefficiency in itself. It is subject to misinterpretation, poor hearing, and it cannot be reread for clarity.**

I am not totally down on meetings in general. As stated above, a weekly staff meeting is beneficial and a great teaching opportunity, properly approached. Additionally, a short meeting to "jump start" an action or project is useful particularly if the staff needs a warning order to prepare for a more formal tasker or to lay out the division of labor necessary to complete a forthcoming tasker.

The real morale busters are the 4:00 p.m. meetings, especially if they are on Fridays! Hubbard's Law, according to a collection of aphorisms by Jerry Gaither, says "The world gets a little better each morning, then worse again in the evening. Hold committee planning meetings in the morning."

Meetings all too frequently lead to personal interaction instead of action. If executives in an organization spend more than a small part of their week in meetings, it is a sure sign of malorganization. Multiple or extended meetings are wasteful of precious time. Thus, use of time is also addressed in Section 26, Marking Time, and Section 27, Someday Isle.

Meetings all too frequently lead to personal interaction instead of action.

SECTION 51

FAINT PRAISE

"There is a difference between hiring character and hiring characters."
Anonymous

"First-rate people hire first-rate people
while second-rate people hire third-rate people."
Dr. Bruce Heilman

One of the most critical functions of senior leaders is the hiring of their organizations' managers and subordinate leaders. When searching for capable people who have star quality, leaders should pay little mind to resumes. Since the candidate probably wrote or at least provided the information for the resume, it has little value except to examine the quality and attention to detail in the narrative. Although the resume may reflect education and experience, it may not define the quality of the experience nor the candidate's character (leaders must recognize the difference between character and characters). As noted earlier, that is why experienced executives move quickly to the references.

Effective leaders and human resources experts recognize *faint praise* in a reference. References that attest to a candidate's *punctuality* and *low absenteeism* and even worse, state that the candidate is a *good worker*, should cause that application to end up in the dead file. The leadership must seek statements that describe star quality such as outstanding, remarkable, incredible, one-of-a-kind, top one percent, and more. Once the leader finds a candidate whose references reflect that kind of star quality, he starts looking for a job fit. Does this person have other credentials that make him a fit for this position or another within the organization? According to Harvey Mackay, once you find a man of star quality, you hire him even if you don't have a place for him.

The leadership must seek statements that describe star quality such as outstanding, remarkable, incredible, one-of-a-kind, top one percent, and more.

The more references the better (I expect three as a minimum). A close examination of several different references will reveal genuine or faint praise. Of course, references are more reliable when written. Some will speak in favor of an average or marginal candidate but hesitate to document such opinions or observations in writing.

I place little confidence in references from friends and ministers. In many cases, neither has observed the candidate in a work environment, although such references can be helpful in character definition. References are best when signed by a former employer or supervisor.

I admire the writings of Dr. Bruce Heilman, World War II Marine, president and chancellor of the University of Richmond. Dr. Heilman concluded that, "First-rate people hire first-rate people; second-rate people hire third-rate people." I believe this is because too much emphasis is placed on whether the hiring party "likes" the candidate. Likeability is rarely a documented credential in the job description, but it is often an overriding factor in hiring by inexperienced leaders and boards.

When seeking new talent for your organization, require written *professional* references, be alert for faint praise, seek star quality, and don't be overwhelmed by personality and humor.

SECTION 52

IMPROMPTU BUT PREPARED

"Extemporaneous speaking should be practiced and cultivated."
Abraham Lincoln

"Many a great orator is simply a great orator."
Robert Lutz

Speakers are only as good as the material they prepare and deliver. Good speakers never cease to collect material. Generally, they are well-read individuals—otherwise, where would they collect their material?

Experienced speakers save anecdotes, stories, quotes, facts, openers, and closers in subject files. They highlight books, making notes in the margins facilitating future reference. Often, they keep a notebook in their car to jot down thoughts and ideas of value while traveling. Over the years their collections are replete with information on topics of interest, enabling them to quickly prepare a speech or "impromptu" remarks. Thus, impromptu presentations are not always impromptu. Occasionally, leaders deliver seemingly impromptu motivational talks that motivate and inspire with much inflection (prevalent among coaches, military leaders, and politicians), but if the truth were known, even these are often prepared in advance.

Impromptu presentations are not always impromptu.

Rarely do experienced speakers give truly extemporaneous presentations, because they anticipate and keep relevant remarks on file in their mind. Even motivational talks seemingly dealing with a unique situation or event have been prepared and filed away in anticipation of a future need. Additionally, tried and true openers and closers are readily available to tailor to the basic message.

Good speakers rehearse their presentations to define their pauses and inflection. It is alright to refer to notes, but unacceptable to read a speech. The amount of study and rehearsal will dictate how much the speaker refers to his notes. The less, the better.

Public speaking is simply another tool in the kit bag of the senior leader. It will not make him successful. However, it will make him a better communicator, a more interesting person, and in most cases one who is admired and viewed as interesting. But, as Robert Lutz reminds us, it does not make one an effective executive.

> **Public speaking is simply another tool in the kit bag of the senior leader.**

In summary, senior leaders should collect the data (openers, closers, motivators, and anecdotes), write, and rehearse, and follow the Boy Scout motto: Be Prepared!

SECTION 53

SELF-EFFICACY

"If you will it, it is not a dream."
Theodor Herzl

"Never make mediocrity feel comfortable."
Steve Jobs

Self-efficacy is a leadership characteristic that is rarely mentioned even by the academicians who study and publish on this ancient art. Self-efficacy describes people who possess confidence, sound judgment, prudence, and courage to make timely and effective decisions that are often unpopular initially. They tend to have strong convictions, initiative, and the *will* to attack mediocrity, observing and examining every opportunity while leaving no idea behind. In short, they possess *practical wisdom* described by English philosopher, Samuel Coleridge as "common sense in an uncommon degree."

> **Self-efficacy describes people who possess confidence, sound judgment, prudence, and courage to make timely and effective decisions that are often unpopular initially.**

Senior leaders with confidence, judgment, and courage pursue change in the face of opposition. Not only do they possess sound judgment, but they believe in their own ability to judge. I recall the story told by Lee Cockerell, former Executive Vice President of Disney World. Explaining to his staff the difficulty in selling change, Lee told

227

how his wife annoyed him by serving green Tabasco sauce with his meatloaf in place of his long-time favorite red Tabasco sauce. His wife insisted Lee try the sauce, which he did and was converted. Lee's demonstrative point to his staff was, "Can you imagine the push back at Tabasco when someone suggested the company produce a green (hot) sauce?"

Senior leaders with confidence, judgment, and courage pursue change in the face of opposition.

In his fascinating book, *A Failure of Nerve*, Edwin Friedman wrote of his experience and observations as a professor, counselor, and a consultant. According to Friedman, his theory of successful leadership is as applicable to parents as presidents. The universal imperative for organizational success, whether family or business, is the presence of a self-differentiated leader (synonymous with self-efficacy as I view it). Not an autocrat, but one who has clear goals, is immune to the swirling emotional processes, and who will take a stand notwithstanding the risk of displeasing other members or workers.

As a small college quarterback, I assumed the authority to call the plays (high school and college) and even audibled off the coach's plays when it didn't fit the defense at the line of scrimmage. Once at Randolph-Macon College, with the score tied at 6-6 (we had never beaten R-M on their field), I waved the extra point kicker off the field, called my own number, and ran the 2 point conversion. Later, with us leading 14-12, I ran in the 2-point conversion again. This time, Coach Keim did not even send in the kicker. He never mentioned me waving off his kicker. In those days, it wasn't called self-efficacy; it was referred to as brash or cocky. Years later, I gave a speech at the Fairfax County Coaches Association where Coach Keim was the Master of Ceremonies. I told this story, and he simply smiled without comment.

How do we recognize leaders who possess the self-efficacy to make the necessary decisions that turn around a floundering company? More importantly, how do we develop such leaders who have this personal characteristic to lead our nation in these challenging days? I remember Colonel Mike Lowe's description of the "three ways leaders develop—those who learn by reading, those who learn by observing, and, finally, those who have to touch the electric fence."

How do we recognize leaders who possess the self-efficacy to make the necessary decisions that turn around a floundering company?

One thing is sure, leaders characterized by self-efficacy will make timely decisions, do not procrastinate, and have the force of will to initiate change notwithstanding the naysayers, foot-draggers, and hesitators seeking one more study and/or consensus from the staff.

SECTION 54

REPETITION – THE IMPERATIVE

"Effective managers repeat their expectations at least once and often three or four times."
Tredal Neeley and Paul Leonardi

"If you aren't teaching your staff, don't kid yourself, you aren't leading them."
Jim Benson

From my earliest days as a high school football and baseball coach to experiences as a military commander in peace and war to my more recent positions as a college and preparatory school president, I have understood the importance of repeating my expectations to my players, Marines, students, and employees. No one could use "I forgot" as an excuse for falling short. Most cadets can quote my frequent admonishments that, "There is no right way to do the wrong thing," (borrowed from Jerry Panas), and "Bad things happen to people who do bad things." I recall well a Sunday School teacher who required us to memorize (lots of repetition) and recite scripture, some of which I remember to this day.

The May 2011 edition of the *Harvard Business Review* reports on research conducted by Tsedal Neeley and Paul Leonardi wherein their research team shadowed thirteen managers in six companies for more than 250 hours. Their findings are interesting, reinforce my thinking relative to redundancy of message, and are as follows:

- Effective managers repeat their expectations at least once and often three or four times. The repetition was deliberate. Some expressed their expectation verbally and then followed up with an email documenting the same message.

- Employees are pulled in different directions by so many mediums of communications that leaders must use repetition to ensure their top messages receive the appropriate priority.

- Results are more timely when the repetition is proactive for emphasis rather than when it is reactive after observing failure of compliance.

Repetition is just as effective in education and in the home as in the workplace. How many times did our parents repeat instructions that we were, apparently, trying to forget? Corporate leaders, military leaders, successful coaches, and all strong leaders use repetition in policy, expectations, and to voice organizational imperatives for success.

Finally, say it once, and it is quickly forgotten. Repeat it often, and it will be remembered and hopefully, become habitual. Repetition is an imperative to ensure important actions are completed for the sake of safety, efficiency, and consistency. The senior leader bears the standard for all three and must frequently say what must be said, when it must be said, and as often as it must be said.

The senior leader bears the standard for all three and must frequently say what must be said, when it must be said, and as often as it must be said.

SECTION 55

COMMITMENT

"Unless commitment is made, there are only promises and hopes, but not plans."
Peter F. Drucker

"It was character that got us out of bed, commitment that moved us to action, and discipline that enabled us to follow through."
Zig Ziglar

The Marines' commitment to their Corps and to one another is widely known, but the depth of that commitment is difficult to imagine unless one experiences it. Senior leaders must seek this same level of commitment from their employees.

Although there are many examples, I will cite one that is unforgettable. It was during the monsoon season in the fall of 1969 when 2nd Platoon, Company "I," 3rd Battalion, 1st Marines was twenty-five or so miles west of Da Nang, alone in a platoon patrol base at the foothills of what was known as "Charlie Ridge" (Charlie was a nickname for the Viet Cong). This was a dangerous area particularly for a platoon of thirty-five to forty-five Marines as it was approximately three to four miles from the remainder of Company "I."

We were in this general location for seven to ten days. We moved every day or two to preclude the Viet Cong from planning an attack on our poorly defended position; poorly defended because we only had some shallow, rain-filled foxholes for cover, and there was little concealment from observation. It never stopped raining during this period, and the only shelter from the misery was our ponchos and shabby hooches rigged out of extra ponchos and canvas shelter halves. We continually fought the temptation to relax our security. No one wanted to man the small perimeter defense, nor participate in the combat patrols, establish the ambushes, or man the observation and listening posts that are critical to local security. Nonetheless, as the platoon commander, it was my responsibility to enforce and frankly demand discipline, ensuring that the Marines were awake during their night watches and that the ambushes and observation or listening posts were alert and monitoring their radios. In this misery, these were truly the days that try men's souls.

The paths and trails we were patrolling led to and from the mountain (Charlie Ridge), and were strewn with red mackerel cans, which were clear and present evidence that we were intruding into Victor Charlie's domain. Charlie's favorite meal was mackerel, rice, and a fermented fish sauce. Since it was next to impossible to sleep, the danger close environment provided a strong incentive for the Marines to stay awake. Corporal punishment for falling asleep was delivered from the squad leaders, platoon sergeant, and right guide. I never observed it, but I knew it was measured and necessary. The weather contributed to absolute misery 24/7. The danger itself demanded commitment, but we still had to enforce unit discipline almost ruthlessly.

In combat, troops often lose track of the date and day of the week; the days are all the same except for an occasional voluntary prayer meeting on Sunday. Even that is hard to organize, because the ambushes and observation or listening posts have returned and troops are trying to get some morning rest; the mud, rain, and misery made it hard to sleep until one reached near exhaustion. By mid-morning and early afternoon the combat patrols were back out.

So on this day, none of us realized that the date was November 10th, the Marine Corps' Birthday—a day many of us would rather celebrate than our own true birth date. In some ways, the date signifies our rebirth and membership in something much greater than our individual selves. This rebirth created a change in what we believed in and what we thought was good enough in terms of effort and achievement. It involves a brotherhood many admire, but few have the courage to join, because the commitment and risks are just too onerous.

Around dusk, one of the observation posts (OP) called in to say that, "two ¼-ton vehicles [jeeps] were slowly approaching with night running lights on." At first, we concluded they couldn't be our vehicles, because it would be reckless and much too dangerous for two vehicles to be at our area of operations (AO) at that hour. There had been no communications from the Company headquarters that friendly vehicles would be in our AO. Could the OP have misidentified the vehicles—the North Vietnamese Army (NVA) and Viet Cong did not have vehicles like ours?

I quickly selected a fire team (four Marines) to move down to the road to see what was approaching—friend or foe? Soon, the team leader reported back that the vehicles were carrying Company Gunnery Sergeant (GySgt) Maloon and five Marines, and they had something for us.

GySgt Maloon was a veteran of thirty-five years in the Corps. He had seen action in Korea and Vietnam. The Gunny was a big man, probably 6 foot 6 inches, more than 250 pounds, and always carried an old Thompson submachine gun. He was gruff and seemingly unfriendly to new lieutenants until they proved their mettle to his satisfaction. In fact, you knew when you had earned his respect, because he would refer to you as lieutenant and maybe even sir on occasion. Before that, he referred to lieutenants as Mr.—in my case, Mr. Benson, which galled me for a while. Nonetheless, I grew to admire the Gunny, and later I sought his counsel on tactical decisions and more.

By the time I moved the platoon to the road, it was essentially dark and time for the ambushes and listening posts to depart our patrol base. To a degree, I put security aside when I realized that the Gunny had spent the day going to every company outpost ensuring that every Marine had hot coffee and U.S. Marine Corps birthday cake. We celebrated as the rain poured down on our party. We laughed and yucked it up the way Marines do in misery. The party was short-lived as the Gunny and his five Marine security force still had a dangerous trip back to Hill 37, which was the location of the 3rd Battalion, 1st Marines command post and our company's rear area that coordinated supplies, administration, casualty reporting and more.

It was on that November 10th that I truly realized what commitment was all about and what made the Marine Corps the great and unique organization it remains today.

SECTION 56

TURNAROUNDS AND RECOVERIES

"God hurries and drives me. I am not master of myself;
I wish to be quiet, but am hurried into a midst of tumults."
Martin Luther

"Mediocra is a non-Webster's noun that describes the
results of democratic decision-making."
Robert Lutz

Turnaround leaders are not legacy leaders per Dr. Mark Rutland. Turnaround leaders create unwanted change, move everyone's cheese (sometimes they take it away), and prepare the organization for the legacy leaders.

Dr. Rutland was known for his work in saving Calvary Church in Orlando, Southeastern University in Lakeland, Florida, and Oral Roberts University. In his fine book, *Relaunch*, he termed turnaround leaders as "gunslingers" who cleanup the town, run off the bad guys, close the saloons, then get on their horse and ride off. According to Dr. Rutland, a turnaround leader normally doesn't have many friends and serves a lonely term of office. When he mounts his horse to ride away, there is relief. Often the workers claim to miss the spouse of the turnaround architect, but little is said regarding the leader who saved their jobs.

Organizations possess three kinds of new leaders. First is the "sustainment leader" who takes over a producing and successful organization. Next is the "recovery leader" who assumes the lead of an under-performing organization—one that needs to revisit its vision, mission, and customers. "A turnaround leader" takes on an organization that has completely lost its direction, is financially unsound, and is heading for bankruptcy without a dramatic makeover.

There is little to be said about the sustainment leader. However, a significant difference exists between the actions of a recovery leader and those of a turnaround leader, and they are worthy of much discussion.[18] Dr. Henry Cloud, in his fine book, *Necessary Endings*, writes that a turnaround leader strategically prunes the organization when the reality of failure is clear and present. I suggest that in a recovery, the leader *prunes* the workforce to better fit his intent and to establish a new direction. In a *turnaround*, the leader *purges* the workforce of the naysayers, half-steppers, stasis defenders, whiners, and other pathogens. The nature of the turnaround process makes the turnaround leader controversial to say the least.

> ## In a turnaround, the leader purges the workforce of the naysayers, half-steppers, stasis defenders, whiners, and other pathogens.

Throughout this book, I have repeated how people resist change and that change creates an unhappy faction in the workforce. Even the best turnaround leaders dread the fallout from their decisions and know that, for a while at least, they will be viewed by others as the enemy. Robert Lutz refers to the *others* as "the dark forces that cling to the status quo." He also reminds us that "dramatic change needs soak time" before it is accepted, but even then it may not be forgiven. To create the kind of change necessary to turn an organization around, the leader requires confidence, strong convictions, great energy, and a *damn the fallout* attitude.

---

18   Cloud's definitions below differ slightly from those of this author. The author's definitions are:
Recovery: make a failing organization successful without changing its basic identity—save what is. turnaround: remake a failing organization into a different organization—make something new.

> ## To create the kind of change necessary to turn an organization around, the leader requires confidence, strong convictions, great energy, and a damn the fallout attitude.

I must say in the beginning that turnaround leaders are not necessarily better leaders than others. They are just better suited to lead dramatically failing organizations—organizations that are already a train wreck or at least the collision is imminent. Moreover, a turnaround leader will need a much deeper understanding of the operating environment of the failing organization so he knows where to take it.

Turnaround leadership is not for all leaders. Those who crave stasis, love, and affirmation, or dislike confrontation, are not the right choice to lead dramatically failing organizations that demand significant change in managers, key staff, strategy, and policies and processes. Nonetheless, I have known many successful leaders who may not have been the right choice for dramatic change, but who excelled in their organization using a steady, grounded, and *seemingly* a more caring form of leadership. In those organizations, loyalty up and down the hierarchy was obvious, and forty to fifty-hour weeks were the norm rather than the sixty to eighty-hour weeks endured in a turnaround. So I cannot say that turnaround leadership is better leadership. But turnaround leadership is what is required in organizations that are failing and boneyard bound.

> ## Turnaround leadership is not for all leaders.

Those who take forlorn organizations and rescue them must be both visionary leaders, knowledgeable about the type and nature of the organization, and conceptual thinkers. As I wrote earlier, they must be able to see the end state and the path to get there. The ability to see the desired end-state and to conceptualize the path to that end state is part of the road to success in a turnaround. But I emphasize, it is only a part of the route.

Those who take forlorn organizations and rescue them must be both visionary leaders, knowledgeable about the type and nature of the organization, and conceptual thinkers.

In the excellent treatise on leadership as an emotional process in his book entitled, *A Failure of Nerve*, the late Edwin Friedman offered that the universal principle of organizational success is the presence of a *well-differentiated leader*. Friedman described this person as "someone who has clarity about his or her own goals, and therefore, "someone who is less likely to become lost in the anxious emotional processes swirling about ... someone who can separate while still remaining concerned, and therefore can maintain a modifying, non-anxious, and sometimes challenging presence ... and be able to take stands at the risk of displeasing."

Friedman also explains the *ever-present* resistance to change that the leader experiences. He calls it sabotage and concludes that "it comes with the (leadership) territory and is characterized by cliques, backbiting, withdrawal, polarization, and subversion." Turnaround leaders experience the above and more!

I suggest that the following are characteristics of successful turnaround leaders that are necessary in lieu of the prevailing tendency for reasonableness, patronization, love, stasis, and consensus building.

Turnaround Leaders Create Turbulent Times:

1. They upset the status quo; they don't just move everyone's cheese. Sometimes, they take it away!

2. They create tension, conflict, and unhappy factions that can undermine their intent and vision.

3. They function poorly within a democratic decision-making environment.

4. They are risk-takers who have a distain for risk-averse decision-making.

5. They are frequent users of the "No" response to batten down the big spenders.

6. They move mediocre, below average, and sometimes even *average* performers to the bench or early retirement.

7. They seek accountability and demand it from staff members.

8. Patience is not their strong suit.

9. They micromanage when losing confidence in a subordinate manager or staff member who is under-performing, and there is a limit of how long this situation will be allowed to exist.

10. They can be irritable and seemingly insensitive leaders who analyze, decide, execute, move on, and never look back.

11. They possess strong convictions and execute in the face of opposition, recognize the consequences, and consider them acceptable.

12. They make pragmatic decisions that are necessary but unpopular and sometimes hurtful to employees *and* their spouses notwithstanding the positive results to the bottom line.

13. They absorb the criticism and shed the gossip and sarcasm.

14. They possess the willingness to face reality and create endings, e.g., programs, policies, and staff mediocrity.

15. They do not measure their decisions on the popularity scale.

These are my 15 characteristics of the turnaround leader. I could have added, often "characterized by self-doubt," because turnaround leaders also have feelings and the necessary decisions and endings create misgivings and doubts for the leader also. Turnaround leadership is not for the faint of heart or the bleeding heart and, for the record, this is not meant to be a political statement. It is only for those who can function in tension and chaos and who do not need nor seek constant affirmation and friendships. They know that the success of the enterprise is more important than their popularity as a leader.

My first turnaround was in my first real job—that of a high school baseball coach at Patrick Henry High School in Roanoke, Virginia. I assumed the position in the winter of 1966 after being a varsity football assistant coach in the fall. It was a program that was relatively new and had yet to experience success. Within two weeks of the start of the season, we were 0-4. But two losses were to the VA Tech freshmen and Staunton Military Academy, a post-high school team. From there, we went 10-6. But with a strong finish and a 10-10 overall record we won the Roanoke City-County Championship and the State Western District Tournament Championship (there were no state playoffs in those days). The next year we won the City-County Championship again, but were runner-up in the District, losing in the finals to a fine George Washington team of Danville, Virginia. That year I was selected as the first ever Roanoke City-County Baseball Coach of The Year. Each successive turnaround became more complex as the following paragraphs portray.

In 1968, I resigned my position at Patrick Henry High School, drove to Richmond, Virginia, and signed up for the U.S. Marine Corps Officer Candidate School (OCS). My intent was to join for four years, go to Vietnam as an infantry platoon commander, and return to coaching. The four years in the Marine Corps turned into twenty-six years, and I soon learned that the Marine Corps was also coaching but with much higher stakes.

My next turnaround was subsequent to completion of my training and commissioning as a Second Lieutenant. I took over command of 2nd Platoon, Company I, 3d Battalion, 1st Marine Regiment in the Republic of South Vietnam, replacing a second lieutenant who had been killed, one of of many casualties incurred in a daylight ambush by the Q82d NVA Regiment. When I assumed command; the platoon was demoralized, without discipline, and led by an alcoholic platoon sergeant. Upon arrival, I was introduced to him by the company commander just as the platoon was departing the company area to establish a platoon patrol base eight to ten kilometers from the company command post. The aforementioned platoon sergeant, who was acting as platoon commander, had an alcohol issue that affected the morale and combat effectiveness of the platoon. Soon I would fire him, write him an adverse performance evaluation, and undo the bad habits, tactics, and procedures he had installed.

In 1980, I was an instructor at the Naval Amphibious School in Little Creek, Virginia, when out of the blue I received a call from Headquarters U.S. Marine Corps to pack up; Mary and I were immediately moving to Camp Pendleton, California, where I would assume command of a separate element of the 1st Air-Naval Gunfire Liaison Company (1st ANGLICO). The company-size command only had about 120 Marines and sailors, but it had a unique mission of calling for and adjusting Marine close air support and naval gunfire for allied and U.S. Army units, and members had to be parachute qualified.

When Mary and I arrived in California, I was advised not to spend time with the existing commander, who had just failed the Commanding General's Inspection, and was ostensibly being relieved of command. The Commanding General, Major General F.X. Quinn, told me the unit was not operationally nor administratively combat ready and would be re-inspected in six weeks.

This was going to be fun; the unit command post was located on the beach, giving us a great venue for physical training where we would soon run four to eight miles in boots and flak jackets in both packed and soft sand. These long runs were for endurance and not speed but built morale and esprit.

More importantly, I quickly learned that operations to the unit essentially meant parachute operations. Jumps were a source of macho braggadocio and extra pay, but tactically it was only a way to get where we could do our primary mission. In this unit, it was about how many jumps were in your logbook and could you land on or near the "T" (target on the ground). No one had any idea what was supposed to happen on the ground and once in the objective area.

The naval gunfire spotters didn't even know the "call for fire." The aviators who served as tactical air officers were solid and knew how to call for and adjust close air support, but being pilots and bombardier/navigators by specialty; they did not know how to organize a field exercise. Other than flying and landing in hostile places in helicopters in Vietnam, an adventure that I could do without, and receiving close air support in a few firefights, I had little experience working with Marine aviators. I preferred my place on the ground with the grunts. I trusted myself more than I trusted man-made equipment, especially helicopters. I well recalled the times in Vietnam and later when there were moments of intense suspense sitting in the back of a CH-46 or CH-53 feeling helpless as the pilot negotiated obstacles or avoided enemy fire.

With an able staff, we were able to change the culture of the unit. We passed the follow-up Commanding General's Inspection and became operationally and administratively proficient while excelling in everything that was measureable to include simple things such as reenlistments and hometown news releases that brought recognition to the young Marines in their first enlistment. Parachute jumping was relegated to a supporting skill, not the driver of our training schedule. Nonetheless, change was not appreciated by some of the veterans of the unit, and unfortunately some personnel pruning was necessary.

I am an admirer of former Marine aviator Robert Lutz, the dauntless former president and vice chairman of Chrysler Corporation and recognized turnaround leader. Lutz is a self-described curmudgeon who, much like Dr. Rutland, has turned every organization he has touched from boneyard-bound to profitability. Lutz argues for courage as the cornerstone of leadership and has little love for what he terms "nominal" or "positional" leaders. He describes them as "no risk" individuals lacking the fortitude to break the status quo and dodging accountability through compromise and shared decision-making (sounds a lot like public and private higher education).

Lutz also described the seemingly thoughtful, articulate, and popular left-brained commander or CEO as one who makes all feel secure and loved in the military and business in less turbulent times. But when all hell breaks out, the economy tanks, and other calamities strike the organization, it is the irascible, right-brained, stasis-breaking leader who has no fear of using the word "No" to button down the big spenders and moving the below average or mediocre performers to the bench, into retirement (early), or off the reservation.

My experience and observation of high-achieving organizations is that tension and conflict are the norm. Larry Bossidy, CEO of Allied Signal Corporation, takes it a step further by writing that, "Tension and conflict are necessary ingredients of successful organizations." Thus, some gentle souls will chaff at the harmony-busting leader who creates change in people and procedures while seeking to improve performance. It seems to me that perfect harmony is absent from high achieving organizations, and if it is present, it can be an indicator of averageness.

My experience and observation of high-achieving organizations is that tension and conflict are the norm.

It must be in my DNA to want to be accountable and succeed or win at everything and that drive has not always led to popularity among some employees and peers. Some have rightfully accused me of micromanaging their departments or divisions. I do have a tendency to micromanage areas wherein I have an intense interest or the subordinate leader is inexperienced, and I lack confidence in the direction or leadership of the department.

A significant part of leader maturation, particularly at the executive level, is the acquisition of the wisdom of knowing when to terminate a subordinate leader, doing it only after careful deliberation, hating the process, and managing the fallout. Executives should have a large front door and a small backdoor, or in time the pushback will be extremely stressful as is usually the case in turnarounds. Leaders must do all ethically possible to find, hire, train, pay, and retain those who create revenue for the organization.

> **Executives should have a large front door and a small backdoor, or in time the pushback will be extremely stressful as is usually the case in turnarounds.**

Subsequent to six months with the 2nd platoon and executing daily and nightly combat patrols and ambushes, I was called up to the 3rd Battalion, 1st Marines S-3 Section (operations). It was standard procedure to bring the infantry lieutenants up to the staff due to the high casualty rate in the field and to exploit the operational knowledge they had gained. Although I hated leaving my platoon and knew I was well-suited for the bush, I was glad to go to the S-3, because it was the heartbeat of the battalion. The role of the S-3 officer or actual, as he was often referred to, was to plan and execute all battalion combat operations. As the new Assistant S-3 (S-3A), I was actually in charge of battalion operations whenever the S-3 officer was resting, off with the battalion commander, or away from the command post (CP). The S-3 was a fine officer, and more importantly, he had the confidence of battalion commander LtCol Thomas P. Ganey. LtCol Ganey was hell on wheels and aggressively enforced all regulations. He would not hesitate to relieve a leader if he perceived the leader was not insisting on good order and discipline and operational excellence.

> **That to turn around a failing organization, it takes a leader with the force of will and personality to make the tough calls, handle the blow back, and persevere—one able to walk point in the defense of his convictions whether they be procedural or moral.**

The S-3 was the only one able to *handle* LtCol Ganey who seemed to shoot from the hip and create unnecessary havoc. If a commander was taking too many casualties and/or not getting sufficient kills, his days were numbered. The other senior officers in the battalion stood clear of the "old man" as he was called.

I was S-3A for only three weeks when the 3rd platoon commander of Company "I" was fired, never to be seen or heard of again. The S-3 officer thanked me for my time in the S-3 shop, but said the "old man" wanted me to go back to India Company and take over 3d platoon. Moreover, things were not well with the company and the company commander's job was in jeopardy. I was glad for the challenge the reassignment presented, and quickly realized that what was once a fine platoon under First Lieutenant Dave Miller was now a danger unto itself. The squad leaders were poorly led and trained, and I don't even remember the platoon sergeant; he made no impression on me whatsoever. Although it was truly a turnaround command, I was unfamiliar with the term in those days. Nonetheless, I made the hard and seemingly unpopular decisions organizationally and tactically and within several weeks, I took pride in how the platoon had jelled. But in hindsight, they were Marines, so why should I have expected anything less?

Soon I was hearing rumors that my previous command, 2nd platoon had fallen on hard times. My successor had been fired and the platoon was being led by the platoon sergeant. Staff Sergeant Zenith Price was the 19th of 19 children from a West Virginia family. He was Benson-trained as he had been my platoon sergeant for five months before I left for the battalion staff. I had complete confidence in Price and was glad to hear that he was now the platoon commander even if it was only until a new lieutenant arrived.

I was approaching the end of my twelve-month tour in Vietnam, when I was called to the battalion command post once more. There, I was told that the new battalion commander had fired the India Company Commander for outrageous misjudgment in the tactical employment of the company, and I was to immediately leave 3rd platoon and assume command of the company. I was well-prepared for the new assignment. I knew the leadership of the 2nd and 3rd platoons and most of the battalion staff. I did not know the leadership in the first platoon.

The company was not as resistant to change as I expected, because the subordinate leaders had completely lost confidence in my predecessor. Soon after taking command, the company was moved to Hill 190, closer to DaNang as the pullout of U.S. forces had begun. Hill 190 was a defensive position with a mess hall and many equipment assets to protect. Our mobility and ability to plan and operate tactically were greatly diminished, and now I had the garrison-type problems associated with a static position and little ability to maneuver against the enemy.

Although our casualties went down significantly, so did our kills, and it was hard to see how we were winning our part of the war. Previously, we had been the point of the spear. We had been twenty-five or so kilometers west of DaNang and often operating independently defeating the enemy day by day with carefully planned patrols, ambushes, and helicopter-borne raids during hamlet/village cordon and search operations. Nonetheless, we adapted to the new mission and were again the respected Company "I" of the past.

In late May 1969, I gave up command of Company "I" and the battalion commander rewarded me with a week of Rest and Recuperation (R&R) in Sydney, Australia.

Dr. Albert Mohler Jr., is the president of the Southern Baptist Theological Seminary, one of the largest seminaries in the world. He is a noted author, sought-after speaker, and has made numerous appearances on national news networks. His work on Christian leadership is applicable to politics, business, education, and more.

In Section eight of Dr. Mohler's book, *The Conviction to Lead*, he explains that contemporary leaders often lack a clear conviction of where they are to take their organization. There seems to be a correlation here with Robert Lutz's nominal or positional leaders and Albert Mohler's leaders without conviction. Mohler's theme is that much of what passes today for leading is nothing more than management of people and material. According to Mohler, "Without convictions you might be able to manage, but you cannot really lead." I would add that to turn around a failing organization, it takes a leader with the force of will and personality to make the tough calls, handle the *blow back*, and persevere—one able to walk point in the defense of his convictions whether they be procedural or moral.

Subsequent to my experience in Vietnam, I had an invigorating military career commanding organizations up to regimental size, with nearly 5,000 Marines and sailors. Generally, I followed competent commanders and department heads who passed on well-led units and departments that didn't require a turnaround approach, but simply had to adjust to my style of leadership and interest.

The one exception was after I joined the United States Southern Command in the Republic of Panama. As a Major having just graduated from the Armed Forces Staff College in Norfolk, Virginia, I was assigned as an American embassy evacuation planner for the high threat embassies in Central and South America, primarily Nicaragua, Honduras, Panama, El Salvador, and Columbia. In Section 3, I wrote about my adventures in contingency/war planning in Nicaragua that far exceeded embassy evacuation planning.

Upon promotion to Lieutenant Colonel and the arrival of Colonel John Spoone, USAF, as the Director of the J-5 Directorate, Strategic Plans and Policy, I was named the Chief of Plans and Force Development for the theater of operations. At that time, the J-5 Directorate had never had a contingency plan approved by the Joint Chiefs of Staff (JCS)! Notwithstanding the fact that the process was cumbersome, replete with compromise due to service rivalries, and required concurrence from all four Services and the JCS, it was unheard of for any Unified Command like the Southern Command not to have approved plans for their theater contingencies.

There were two Nicaragua contingency plans that were considered top secret and a very high priority for completion. Others for Panama and other high threat countries had been in the works for years. The previous Director of J-5 was known as a master "word-smither" with little conceptual ability, so year after year the plans rarely got out of the headquarters to be considered for JCS approval, and when they did, they were returned with numerous reasons for rejection. I don't know if the plan failures were the demise of the previous Director or not, but the priority of plan completion changed dramatically with the arrival of Col John Spoone as the Director of J-5.

Without going through the specifics of service parochialism—characterized by varying degrees of gossip, jealousy, reluctant compromise, and even cooperation from the subordinate command planners—thanks to the audacity and force of will on the part of Colonel Spoone and General Jack Galvin, Commander-in-Chief of The Southern Command (CINCSOUTH), seven plans were approved by the JCS in approximately eighteen months. This was truly a turnaround for a department that heretofore had nothing to crow about other than exotic travel, cheap liquor, and exquisite cuisine in beautiful but dangerous Latin American countries. Admittedly, I was the author or editor of each of those plans and received two decorations (Medals) in that eighteen-month period as acknowledgement for my efforts.

In the early 1990s, while serving as the Chief of Staff and Assistant Division Commander for the 16,000-man 2nd Marine Division under the excellent leadership of Major General Butch Neal, the Division Staff Judge Advocate reported to the General, but he and his twelve or more lawyers essentially worked for me. The Staff Judge Advocate was a Colonel and a fine Marine, but his bevy of lawyers were mostly young captains and majors who, other than the uniform, might not be selected from a crowd as Marine officers. Their briefings to the General could leave me apoplectic. Notwithstanding my instruction and even demonstration of the modified position of attention, use of the pointer while briefing, and military briefing techniques, some would invariably brief with their arms and the pointer nervously flailing about, speak too fast using their hands as if they were attached to their mandible, interrupt the General in the middle of his questions, and display no concept of military bearing. Finally, I instructed the lawyers when they briefed the General to look at me (I sat on the right of the General), not him. They would know by my expression how they were doing. The madder I got, the more nervous they became. Moreover, I had hand signals for them. With my hand to my face opposite the General, one finger up meant slowdown, two fingers up meant speed up, and three fingers up meant sit down. For reasons I don't recall, the Staff Judge Advocate was travelling frequently, and I spent a lot of time counseling and editing the work of his lawyers. Not only was I unimpressed with their military bearing, I was less impressed with their writing skills. As the Chief of Staff for the 400-man Division Staff, I was exacting and insufferable. I knew well that the efficiency of the staff was much more important than my popularity, and those lawyers surely had a distain for one Colonel Benson.

Upon departure from the great 2nd Marine Division, I joined the Navy's 2nd Fleet Staff on board the U.S.S. Mount Whitney. It was a boring and monotonous year as one of three Marines on the ship. I have a great respect for the U.S. Navy and previously experienced two wonderful years as the Commanding Officer of the Marine Detachment onboard the U.S.S. Oklahoma City, the flagship of the 7th Fleet. However, my year on the Mount Whitney was spent mostly at anchor off the coast of Haiti in humanitarian operations. Upon return to the U.S. in December of 1994, I was invited to return to Bridgewater College to help the new president find a head football coach. I was delighted to go and spend three days with my college friend Dr. Phillip C. Stone, president, interviewing candidates and discussing his vision of change for the college.

Phil Stone had been a classmate at Bridgewater and had early on showed a propensity to lead. He was not an athlete himself, but had an avid interest in athletics. We ran in a different crowd—mine much more rowdy and non-observant of the College's strict behavioral rules. The one time we did get rowdy together, we ended up on disciplinary probation for a semester.

During our three days together, we discovered that we had similar philosophies for leading and resurrecting a college that had been listing to the portside with stalled enrollment growth, low student morale, and possessing a few departments with much to be modest about. I decided to retire from the Marine Corps and move to Bridgewater to be his Executive Assistant and Director of Planning.

Phil was a very successful lawyer before assuming the presidency of the college. At the time, I remember thinking that those lawyers in the 2nd Marine Division whom I had so abused were now laughing in their cups that that SOB Benson was now working for a lawyer.

When Phil took over at Bridgewater, it was not failing like some organizations I would encounter later. Thus, I would not classify it as a turnaround project requiring drastic change. However, it needed surgery and recovery time. The academic departments and maintenance departments were very good. The people in admissions and financial aid and athletics were good, but they were under-staffed, under-funded, and needed a new set of expectations. The fundraising arm was failing, and a $60M capital campaign was floundering. The student development department was overly provincial and too over-bearing for the society from which the student population emanated.

Phil Stone, bolstered by his experience as a Bridgewater board of trustee member, was armed with the information and leadership tools to right the ship. His upbeat, caring personality rallied the faculty and staff and elevated student morale that would soon cause a dramatic increase in student retention.

Changes in his expectations and replacement of some personnel in a historically unsuccessful athletic department soon led to a thirty-six game Old Dominion Athletic Conference football winning streak and a NCAA Division III heartbreaking loss for the National Championship in Salem, Virginia. Moreover, the college won the Old Dominion Athletic Conference Commissioner's Cup for overall athletic superiority. Meanwhile, over a period of six or so years, applications grew from approximately 950 to more than 2200. Not only was the $60M capital campaign completed, but another $5.5M campaign was completed less than one year after its announcement and was used to build a beautiful new Wellness and Recreation Center.

Soon thereafter, the funds were raised to construct an $8.2M apartment-style dormitory to house the rapidly expanding population. After three years as the Executive Assistant to the President and Director of Planning, I assumed the newly created position of Vice President of Administration wherein I was accountable for virtually all departments except the Business Office, Academic Affairs, and Development (fundraising).

Although I was anything but the spearhead behind the recovery at Bridgewater College, it was a powerful learning platform for what I was to face in 2004 when I assumed the presidency of Marion Military Institute (MMI) in Marion, Alabama.

MMI was a military two-year college and preparatory school that had been a school or college since 1842 and a military two-year college and preparatory school since 1887. Buildings dating back to 1864 were fragile and still in daily use. The preparatory high school, grades nine through twelve, co-existed with the college and some teachers/professors taught at both levels.

The Institute was plagued with a pending lawsuit by the alumni who were not permitted by the Institute's president to come on campus as a group. This litigation had been ongoing for more than two years with the anger and ill-feelings seriously affecting fundraising and alumni support. Working with a new board chairman and a well-intentioned chairman of the alumni association, I wrote and negotiated an affiliation agreement that brought the alumni back on campus with two seats on the Board of Trustees. I traveled extensively winning the hearts and minds of the same alumni who had funded the lawsuit. Soon, fundraising increased dramatically, homecoming attendance grew exponentially, and the lawsuit was discontinued.

When I arrived, the grass had grown over the curbs and well onto the sidewalks. A rain gutter was hanging down from the front of the Administration Building and was illustrative of what parents and prospective cadets would see when they visited the campus for the first time. I could find no evidence whatsoever that any building had been painted in the previous twenty years. Although the debt was less than $3M, the endowment had been spent down to $800K.

But worst of all, soon after I arrived, the college had completed the first phase of its Southern Association of Colleges and Schools (SACS) reaccreditation inspection that revealed twenty-two non-compliant areas. I had never heard of such a dismal performance. Having just endured a successful workup and completion of a reaccreditation at Bridgewater, I knew well what was ahead. We were allotted six weeks to correct the discrepancies before the SACS team would arrive to see if these areas had been brought into compliance. I had little hope of repairing all of the non-compliant areas as some of the processes were required to have been in place for one year! My only hope was to achieve probation, which would allow us a year to develop and implement the procedures that were absent but required in order to protect our federal funding. After six incredible weeks of administration that included my firing of the previously selected Director of Reaccreditation, the visiting SACS team arrived for their three-day visit.

The reaccreditation team was led by a very professional two-year college president from Gainesville, Georgia, and after three days of detailed inspection and analysis, we escaped with a "Warning," which was better than "Probation" and gave us until the next summer to bring a few remaining processes into SACS compliance. Breathing a sigh of relief, the Board was elated, and the next summer the Institute received its reaffirmation of accreditation.

The Institute's Board of Trustees had repeatedly failed to understand the importance of hiring an experienced businessman as president. Like so many other private, independent military schools, they had repeatedly hired superb, successful military leaders who had never had to make a payroll, create a profit margin, deal with the whims and needs of a faculty, co-exist with a Board of Trustees who are often Type-A individuals in their own right, or endured an arduous reaccreditation. Four presidents before me had departed under dire conditions.

Other challenges not initially observed were the remaining racially-polarized politics and poverty in the town of Marion and Perry County. The public schools were so depressing that few families with school-aged children would consider moving into the town. The lone private K-12 school wasn't much better. I was prepared to remove the staff and teachers who were less than effective, but replacing them was a continuous headache. The Academic Dean and Commandant were the first to go. I was able to hire a first-rate Dean, but I suffered with a disloyal and incompetent Commandant for three years before I was able to find and hire the right officer. I was very fortunate to find a superb Director of Development who helped me raise $8M in five years and a Director of Admissions to fill the beds to capacity. With the increased revenue, we were able to upgrade the faculty, administration, and coaching staff and achieve what Marine Colonel Hank Stackpole referred to as *balanced excellence*.

We doubled the size of the Board of Trustees and added a fifty-two-member Board of Visitors (often called advisors). The Alumni Association became energized, and our fundraising and alumni affairs officers worked hard to overcome the bad blood that had resulted in the alumni lawsuit against the Board and Administration.

To deal with the decades of deferred maintenance, I travelled wherever alumni existed including the capitol in Montgomery and wherever else we had a considerable number of influential alumni. In an attempt to energize the alumni and other donors, I shared my vision that Marion Military Institute would someday be The Citadel of the state of Alabama—after all, as the only military college in Alabama with 106 acres, twenty-five plus facilities and a distinct heritage, why not?

The serendipitous offshoot was that an alumnus who was a lobbyist in Montgomery explained my vision to Dr. Roy Johnson, the Chancellor of Post-Secondary Education and a former legislator with considerable influence in the state. Dr. Johnson responded that he would be interested in bringing MMI into the two-year college system and could bring considerable resources to the Institute. Dr. Johnson's influence was far greater than we envisioned, and subsequent to many meetings and lobbying all over the state, we had created the legislation (I wrote, Dr. Johnson edited, and the Board of Trustees approved). The bill achieved an overwhelming vote of approval in the Alabama House and Senate and was signed into law by Governor Bob Riley nine months after the initial discussions.

This is a truly truncated version of the challenges we faced that year, but the fact remains that MMI has a bright future. The quality of its Administration and faculty is evidenced by the eighty to ninety cadets who annually complete the MMI Service Academy Preparatory Program and are admitted to one of the nation's military academies—a number unmatched by any preparatory school or two-year college in America. Unfortunately, Dr. Johnson was prosecuted for nepotism related charges and more, shortly after the Institute became a state two-year college. I testified on his behalf before a federal grand jury to no avail as he pled guilty to lesser charges. Nonetheless, during my year working with him, I found Dr. Johnson to be an astute politician and a self-differentiated leader as described by Edwin Friedman, his book, *The Failure of Nerve*. Dr. Johnson followed through on every promise and always had the state and two-year college system's best interest in mind. He was a leader with vision, persuasion, inordinate drive, and persistence who got things done that no one else in the state hierarchy could have achieved.

The acquisition of MMI by the state of Alabama was a no-brainer. The state acquired a valuable, unique, and historical college wherein two of its daily-use buildings served as the Breckenridge Hospital during the Civil War. On the other side of the coin, the MMI Board and alumni ensured the longevity of a college that could have been in the boneyard with the next hurricane, tornado, or failed leader.

MMI became a state-owned institution in the summer of 2006. We spent millions over the next three years restoring the facilities while we dramatically increased enrollment and fundraising. MMI was a legitimate turnaround that was accomplished with the leadership of a dedicated and generous Board of Trustees, a professional staff and faculty, caring alumni, and a wonderful community that genuinely cared about the survival and longevity of its MMI. My contribution was to recognize the problems, communicate my commitment, and execute the unpleasant aspects of necessary change. I rebuilt the staff, changed the standards and expectations, demanded excellence and accountability, and knew when it was time to turn over the reins to a new president with a new vision for a new era.

From the first meeting with the other two-year college presidents, I felt the resentment of our presence in the system. Moreover, the new chancellor who replaced Dr. Johnson thought the legislation was a bad idea and publically said so in both the Montgomery and Birmingham newspapers. Of course, I publicly disagreed with him, and thus got myself at cross purposes with some members of the State Board of Education to whom the new Chancellor reported. Nonetheless, my Board (formerly Board of Trustees but now Board of Advisors) backed me completely, and "some bored with a pretty big auger,'" as Board Chairman Red Wilkins often said. During the three year period from 2006-2009, none of the three chancellors to whom I reported had the leadership, drive, and influence of Dr. Johnson!

Although relations with the other college presidents gradually improved, the fact remained that MMI was a military college and few of the other college presidents understood its purpose and value to the Alabama two-year college system, and all felt the reductions in their budgets caused by the MMI funding being spread-loaded among the other colleges. The frequent trips to Montgomery for Board of Education meetings that had little to do with MMI, the weak-knee leadership from the Chancellor's office, and the friction remaining from the 2006 public debate with the Chancellor (who had since been terminated by the State Board of Education), caused me to question my future at MMI. I began to believe that there really is a shelf-life for turnaround presidents. With help from the Board of Trustees/Advisors, the alumni, and Dr. Johnson, the future of Marion Military Institute had been assured. With a robust enrollment, loyal and supportive alumni, and successful fundraising, MMI was not dependent on my presence—time to move on.

I was heading towards completion of my fifth year at the helm of MMI when I was approached about the presidency of Riverside Military Academy. At first, I had no interest, but after the third invitation I agreed to go to Gainesville, Georgia, to see this 102-year-old military college preparatory school that had undergone a $95M renovation but was failing miserably and possibly headed for sale or bankruptcy.

I had great trepidation about even visiting this Academy because of the incredible support I had received from the MMI Board and its alumni. Moreover, the Board members had just written checks to seed "The James H. and Mary V. Benson Scholarship Fund," which was a significant honor, for which we were very grateful.

In December 2008, I visited the Riverside campus, observed the disorder and absence of military discipline within the corps of cadets, and spoke with members of the executive staff (commandant/ dean of students, academic dean, chief financial officer, director of marketing, director of development, admissions staff, and the deputy superintendent). It was clear that painful decisions would have to be made. During the interview process, I had some time with the departing superintendent (the Board had decided to change the position title to president) who was a good and decent man who had an impressive military career but no preparation for the financial, enrollment, and fundraising challenges inherent in being the chief executive officer of a private academy. It appeared that the Academy was being managed and administered by the deputy superintendent who had never served in the military and was less qualified to administer the Academy than the superintendent himself. There was simply no operational area that I found redeeming. This would not be a recovery or repair; but a major turnaround involving a staff purge and more.

I accepted the offer of the Riverside presidency, and by the time I arrived in June, 2009, the astute Board of Trustees had terminated the deputy superintendent and the director of admissions. On Day 1, I terminated the ill-prepared academic dean, the commandant, and the director of development. Unlike Marion, Gainesville was a thriving city of 35,000, an hour from Atlanta. So there existed a robust pool of applicants to fill any vacancy made in the faculty or staff.

The Board of Trustees had been very transparent relative to the financial situation. I was aware that the Academy was losing $3-5M each year due to over-spending and six consecutive years of decreasing enrollment. The Academy had completed a $95M campus teardown and rebuild from 1997-2004 that was supposed to solve the enrollment problem, but the decline continued and the $132M endowment had been depleted to $83M. The debt incurred in the rebuild totaled more than $83M, and the annual debt service was approximately $5.1M, which was significant considering the revenue history of the Academy.

Two months before I was to assume the Riverside presidency, the Academy's endowment lost almost $30M in the equity market, which put the *debt versus endowment ratio* upside down to the tune of $82M debt and $53M endowment. In time the endowment would recover slightly but not significantly. The headwinds and minefields were daunting, but as I arrived on June 1, 2009, I was eager to take them on. I view every challenge in terms of an opportunity—the passion to have the best team, the best military unit, the best college, or the best academy drove my daily life as I sought excellence across the spectrum of my interests and activities. I had complete confidence that through personal will, knowledge and experience, audacity, and my religious convictions I would be able to turn the organization. However, I also recognized that once the turnaround was accomplished, it might require someone else to sustain it as I would begin to look around for "the next hill to seize" as the chief financial officer at Bridgewater College stated when I departed there in 2004.

At Marion Military Institute and Riverside, the replacements I selected didn't always work out, and I sometimes had to eat crow and replace the replacements. If we are honest with ourselves, only 60-70 percent of our new hires turn out to be all we hoped they would be. Too often we compound the initial mistake by staying with a failed replacement too long. Permitting feelings to interfere with rational, common sense decisions suggests the absence of executive courage.

At the end of my sixth year at Riverside, we had filled 97 percent of the 540 beds, despite the recession and a tuition that exceeded $30K per year. Our revenue increased from $9.9M in 2009 to $19.1M in

2015, an increase of 48 percent. Meanwhile, our expenses increased from \$12.9M to \$15M an increase of 14 percent. We increased tuition 4 percent for five consecutive years, and faculty and staff pay increases totaled 12.5 percent for the period. For the period 2012 to 2015 operational revenues exceeded expenses that included the \$5.1M in debt service.

During my six years at Riverside, I fit Dr. Mark Rutland's description of the *lonely gunslinger* who has to run off the bad guys (in truth, many are good guys, just not the right fit for the organization at the time), make the unpopular decisions, change the foundational policies and procedures, cut the budgets, raise the standards, and hold the subordinate leaders accountable. The gunslinger or turnaround leader will manage multiple crises that often create ill-will, resentment, and much second guessing. Homeostasis will have been tossed out the door as he creates internal crises while managing the external crises. Turnarounds like Marion and Riverside take a toll on the leader, his family, his health, and at times his ego.

Turnarounds like Marion and Riverside take a toll on the leader, his family, his health, and at times his ego.

Whenever I have been frustrated, annoyed, and dissatisfied with my position and my boss, it has been when I worked for what Friedman called a *middler*. A middler is a risk-avoider, one who thrives on creating good feelings, and avoids conflict. He seeks to be a friend of everyone, a "good guy." He is everyone's pleaser and likes to talk tough about action but can't take any, because he must remove all the risk before acting. Unfortunately, this leader is often the brightest and most articulate individual in the room. In some cases, he will become the CEO or a Flag/General Officer. I get reflux and shudder when I think of some for whom I have worked.

Robert Lutz describes the dark forces in organizations that cling to the status quo as those who make the lives of the poets of change and progress miserable. In the face of these dark forces, the turnaround leader can be viewed as irascible, stubborn, hip-shooting but hopefully, convicted, and transparent. Transparency is important, because the change-maker must be understood, trusted, and respected, even if not welcome. The changes are going to create an unhappy faction, and the change-maker will eventually feel diminished and ride off into the sunset per Rutland. Hence, the savior of the organization will rarely stay long enough to enjoy the payoff of his work. I suspect that the nature of the turnaround leader is that he may be too restless and action-focused to enjoy routine, day to day, repetitive operations that should follow a successful turnaround.

> **The changes are going to create an unhappy faction, and the change-maker will eventually feel diminished and ride off into the sunset.**

The turnaround leader reminds me of the parable in Matthew 25:50, which describes the master who gave three servants five, two, and one talent, according to his ability, to maintain while he travelled. When he returned, he found the first two servants had doubled what they had been given, but the third, fearing he would lose the one talent he had been given, buried it. The master dismissed the third servant. I believe this parable defines the Almighty's expectation of the leader when given the opportunity to save a floundering organization. Seeking to maintain the status quo without bold new initiatives, avoiding risk, and the absence of the courage and force of personality to make the hard and often painful decisions are recipes for dismissal and more—just like the third servant.

The turnaround leader, more than any of the others, must frequently walk point. He must stand alone out front, defy the odds against him, dismiss the gossip and criticism, and make decisions often with inadequate information; he simply can't bury the third talent.

SECTION 57

SPIZZERINCTUM

*"When you have done everything you were told to do, you should tell the Master,
'We are unworthy as we have done only what we were told to do.'"*
Luke 17:10

As a high school student-athlete—more athlete than student—in football and baseball in Roanoke, Virginia, we played cross-town rival Andrew Lewis High School in all sports. During my era, we regularly defeated them in all sports except track and field. In track and field, they would devour us with scores of 120 to 15 or something similar.

I remember in a City-County Championship meet, the Andrew Lewis coach running around the inside of the track loudly encouraging his sprinters in the 440 meter race. I would soon learn that his name was Ray Bussard. Later, I would learn that Coach Bussard had left Andrew Lewis and taken a football and track coaching position at Red Bank High School in Chattanooga, Tennessee.

After high school, I enrolled at Bridgewater College and learned that Ray Bussard and Olympic Gold Medal winner Bob Richards had both attended Bridgewater and were winners of the National AAU Best All-Around Track and Field award that was the precursor to the Decathlon. Bussard was a three-sport star at Bridgewater with quite a reputation.

Years later I returned to Bridgewater College as an administrator reporting to the president of the college. Unbeknownst to me and years before, Coach Bussard had departed Red Bank High School, become the head swimming coach at The University of Tennessee, and was viewed by many at his retirement as one of the greatest coaches in Tennessee history.

When I arrived at Bridgewater in 1995, one of my first visitors was Coach Bussard. He had learned that Dr. Phil Stone, the college president, had hired a Marine colonel and that the athletic director reported to him. He sensed that I might be the person he could influence to help turn around a historically mediocre athletic program. Ray and I quickly developed a friendship that would last until his untimely death in 2010.

The more I learned and read about Coach Bussard's accomplishments, beginning with his extraordinary high school coaching record in the Virginia Shenandoah Valley, the more I realized that he possessed the heart of a lion and a passion for winning unlike any I had ever observed.

He was a conceptual thinker who thought strategically (big picture, years out) and tactically (here and now) simultaneously. He had more ideas and gimmicks than I could deal with, and he expected that I would inform the Bridgewater coaching staff and influence implementation of each. Some of Coach Bussard's ideas were useful, but many did not fit into our coaches' scheme of things.

Coach Bussard would be considered meddlesome by some of our coaching staff, and thus, they would often not pay him the deference he deserved. This bothered me, because none of us could hold a candle to Coach Bussard in terms of ability to motivate teams to victory.

At Coach and Ruth Bussard's 50th wedding anniversary, a Knoxville News Sentinel sportswriter told me that Tennessee Athletic Director Bob Woodard hired Coach Bussard in 1967 to ensure no one drowned in the University pool. To everyone's surprise, within two years Coach Bussard had run up a 12-0 SEC record in dual meets and a year later, was named NCAA swim coach of the year. This was only the beginning.

Coach Bussard retired in 1988 after twenty-one years of unparalleled success at Tennessee. His record in dual meets was 252 wins and 20 losses; he won 98 of his first 100 dual meets in the tough Southeastern Conference. He won Southeastern Conference championships, an NCAA title, and he had never coached swimming until he accepted the position of Head Swimming Coach at Tennessee!

I was honored when Coach Bussard invited me to speak at he and Ruth's 50th wedding anniversary at the Homestead in Bath County, Virginia. He invited me to come early before the fifty or so other guests arrived as he wanted to show me where he grew up. I arrived around noon and Ruth fixed us a light lunch and before we went out to get in the 1989 Oldsmobile that the University gave him at retirement, Ray wanted a drink. He gulped down two shots of Jack Daniels Black Label and off we went.

I have been in Vietnam firefights that were less scary than that ninety-minute ride around the ridgelines of Bath County. There were no guard rails and the drop offs seemed endless as I often could not see the bottom of the rocky ravines that we were two to three feet from us at forty-five to fifty miles per hour. Worse than that, Coach Bussard was looking and pointing at everything except the road. When the car veered off on to the gravel shoulder, he would jerk the steering wheel to the left, quickly look ahead, grunt, and continue his story. He had no fear or thought of the "what if"!

I was relieved as we came into a valley, and Coach said he wanted to show me the Boler pool. It was purportedly spring water that had properties that contributed to longevity and other capacities that have escaped my memory. As we pulled in, I observed the very small pool closed off by yellow engineer tape labeled caution. Coach says, "Come on, we are going for a swim!"

"I am not going for a swim, and I didn't bring a suit," I responded.

Immediately, Coach Bussard opened the trunk and tossed me a box a little larger than a toothpaste box inscribed Speedo (meant nothing to me at the time). I opened the box and pulled out this obscene little red and blue bikini-like suit as thoughts raced through my mind—what if someone drove by and saw two old coots cavorting around in a bikini in this off limits, danger-marked, so-called pool?

Coach said the pool stayed at 68°. It felt like 30°. Moreover, the bottom was slimy with moss and rotten leaves and the surface was the home of water spiders and other unfamiliar insects. Coach Bussard stood in the pool waist deep without any concern about the temperature; he never quit telling stories. Meanwhile, I was freezing, swimming back and forth contributing zero to the conversation. I was swimming to try to keep warm, but that never crossed Coach's mind. He thought I was enjoying the workout! After about an hour, we headed back to the house. Ruth was anxious as we were pressing the banquet hour, and we both had to clean up and dress.

At the banquet, I told the story of the afternoon. To ensure that everyone understood the humility I had endured at the pool, I pulled out the still wet Speedo and explained my dilemma at first sight and asking Coach, "Where does the rest of me go?" The audience got it, but I don't think Coach Bussard ever did.

By the time I departed Bridgewater College for the presidency of Marion Military Institute, Coach Bussard was already in the Bridgewater College Sports Hall of Fame, the Greater Knoxville Sports Hall of Fame, the Tennessee Sports Hall of Fame, and the International Swimming Hall of Fame. Soon thereafter, he was selected as one of the 11 University of Tennessee Sports Legends.

A favorite word in Coach Bussard's vocabulary was spizzerinctum. He used it to describe indomitable people. If he said someone had spizzerinctum, it was his highest compliment. Some old dictionaries described it as slang meaning determination, ambition, pride, and the will to succeed. No one I have ever known had more spizzerinctum than Coach Bussard.

> **If Coach said someone had spizzerinctum, it was his highest compliment. Some old dictionaries described it as slang meaning determination, ambition, pride, and the will to succeed. No one I have ever known had more spizzerinctum than Coach Bussard.**

As I described in Section 56, Turnarounds and Recoveries, Coach Bussard was a turnaround specialist. From small high schools to a major Division I university, Coach Bussard changed things that were bad, fixed things that were broken, and corrected things that were wrong. He had no time for left-brain bean counters, naysayers, foot draggers, half-steppers, and second guessers. He was too busy winning to tolerate those in the way of his success. Yes, he created chaos and a lot of it.

Some say that Coach Bussard's insistence on equal treatment for his athletes, internal quarrels, ownership of the practice schedule in the university's natatorium, and more, created headaches from the office of the Tennessee athletic director to the president of the university. Notwithstanding the turmoil he caused, he put Tennessee swimming on the map and changed the swimming legacy of the entire Southeastern Conference. Coach Bussard "made stress nervous" with his demanding practices; acceptance of nothing less than first. There was often friction and confrontation with players, other coaches, and administrators. He retired at fifty-nine years of age, a victim of the turmoil that he himself created.

> ## Coach Bussard "made stress nervous" with his demanding practices; acceptance of nothing less than first.

Some described Coach Bussard as crazy, impossible, intense, cunning, indomitable, a sophisticated unsophisticate, intimidating, and more. Others described him as compassionate, rugged, honest, generous, brilliant, inspirational, spiritual, and the best friend ever.

If there was ever one who possessed moral, physical, and executive courage, it was Ray Bussard. I was fortunate to be his friend, admirer, and even defender in some company. One thing is sure, he was no fun to compete against in anything. Once he gave me a leather key chain inscribed AAA-O, meaning—*anybody, anyplace, anytime, bar none*. It was his way of throwing down the challenge. There is no better example of executive courage than that of Ray Bussard, nor is there a better example of how executive courage and force of will can create havoc with relationships causing varying degrees of internal stress and self-doubt. But the results of Coach Bussard's leadership and willingness to walk point in the face of criticism and second guessing speak for themselves. He is a memorable friend whom I hold in high regard with leadership characteristics that I have never observed before or since.

SECTION 58

LEADERS, ADMINISTRATORS, AND BOTH

"... if the trumpet does not sound a clear call, who will be
ready for battle?"
1 Corinthians 14:8

There is another dimension to leading and winning that is rarely, if ever, addressed in the vast literature on leadership and winning, and that dimension is administration. Because of its heritage, culture, and leader training, the Marine Corps is blessed with superior leaders. My experience has been that despite their leadership ability, some could not administer. I have known superior leaders who were poor administrators and superior administrators who were poor leaders. Those who were both superior leaders and superior administrators connected the dots and cross the Ts. They possessed organizational skills, follow-through characteristics, writing skills, and planning ability. Through internal or developed systems, they could track the status of projects, fulfill promises, document their procedures and regulations, and communicate their intent and tasking in clear and not to be misconstrued prose. Leaders with organizational and administrative skills seemingly never failed an inspection.

I have known superior leaders who were poor administrators and superior administrators who were poor leaders.

When interviewing candidates for division or department head positions, deanships, and other high level positions, I ask a question like, "I am confident you can lead this department, but can you administer it, and if so, what gives you confidence that you can do so?" While in the Marines and later as a senior administrator in higher and secondary education, I followed six senior leaders who were terminated for cause. I don't believe that any of the six were terminated for lack of leadership. But in each case as I seized the reins of the organization, the absence of effective administration was apparent. I had to rewrite or cause to be written virtually every policy and regulation. Usually there was a significant difference between what was written to be done and what, in fact, was being done.

I would sometimes conclude that it would be easier to throw everything out and start over than to fix what was present. Academicians would ask me for evidence of the above and a rational definition of what constitutes administration, and I would have to say that it is anecdotal.

Each year a large number of professional and college football coaches are fired. I know that most are superior leaders. What is missing? I suspect that the absence of administrative skills plays a role in their demise. My battalion commander in Vietnam would repeatedly tell his company commanders that, "If we take care of the little things, the big things will take care of themselves." Quite often the little things were administrative.

Executive leadership is for the most part administrative. I have known charismatic leaders who were admired, even loved, but never reached the pinnacle of success in their field. In most cases, the cause of failure was either moral or administrative.

Executive leadership is for the most part administrative.

I will close by quoting from General Patton's *War as I Knew It*. "Administrative discipline is the index of combat discipline. Any commander who is unwilling or unable to enforce administrative discipline will be incapable of enforcing combat discipline. An experienced officer can tell by a very cursory inspection of any unit (organization), the caliber of its commanding officer (CEO, department head, manager, etcetera)."

SECTION 59

SINE QUA NONS

*"He who reigns within himself, and rules his passions,
desires and fears is more than a king."*
John Milton

"I made my choices and my choices made me."
Reverend Jentzen Franklin

In reading Darren Hardy's fine little book entitled *The Compound Effect*, I was intrigued by his admonition that our daily habits and choices determine how we live, prosper, and experience happiness. According to Hardy, these daily decisions shape our destiny. He calls them *underlying fundamental truths*.

Some years ago, I wrote what I considered the *sine qua nons* of success in work and life. Some would call these leadership corollaries or maxims. I now call them the *sine qua nons* of Leadership. Those who recall their Latin will know that the *sine qua nons* are the indispensable things. If you will, here are my top ten:

1. It has been said that leaders should not suffer fools. I suggest that one can suffer fools longer than one should suffer disloyalty or dishonesty.

2. Employee morale is the oxygen of the organization—plan for it.

3. Establish high standards or expectations for the work force. They will work better at full stretch. Remember the Wilson Pickett tune, "99½ won't do, got to have 100!"

4. Do not debate the importance of *form versus substance*; you must have both. Part of being good is looking good—that applies to your person, your grounds, and your facilities.

Part of being good is looking good—

---

5. Tithe to learning—Give at least 10 percent of your time to professional development, whether it is professional education, individual study, or just plain reading.

Tithe to learning—

---

6. There is a difference between being in control and being controlling. Know the difference and refrain from the latter.

7. When in doubt, trust your instincts, decide, act and don't look back.

8. You must possess self-awareness. *Display* your strengths. *Hide* your weaknesses as you work diligently to eliminate them.

9. Associate with others who possess character and high personal values; bring no one into your confidence who does not possess both.

10. Remember, when you are in charge; you are accountable. Wisdom, supervision, and correction are preludes to success. A great army general once told me, "In God I Trust—everything else I check."

Remember, when you are in charge; you are accountable.

These are the indispensable things that over time create victories in the office, on the battlefield, or playing field. Review them, employ them, advocate them among your followers, and lead, lead, lead.

SECTION 60

CLOSURE

"Leadership is about how to be, not how to do."
Frances Hesselbein

I have been fortunate to lead, develop, and educate America's youth in two widely different fields of endeavor—the battlefield and the corner office. The leadership challenges vary considerably, but they are surprisingly similar when one considers how organizations tend to respond and behave given the leader's intent and style.

My transition from leader-warrior to businessman-educator would be incomplete without the opportunity to reflect on my experiences, failures, and successes. I still miss the leadership challenges and adrenaline rush of the U.S. Marine Corps. But even as a senior educator and businessman, leadership is a complex phenomenon that requires one to stand alone. It also has a selfish and self-centered component. Hopefully, the pages herein help my readers identify these components and turn from selfness to otherness.

Leadership is a complex phenomenon that requires one to stand alone.

James Kouzes and Barry Posner wrote a helpful book entitled, *The Leadership Challenge*. In the book, they told the story of U.S. Army General John Sanford who grew up poor, failed the 6th grade, but went on to graduate from Penn State University on an ROTC scholarship. General Sanford served in Korea, Vietnam, and the first Persian Gulf War. Later he served as a county manager in Fulton County, Georgia, and the superintendent of the public schools in Seattle, Washington. In response to an interview question about his secret to successful leadership, he replied it was "love" that gave him the ability to inspire others. He loved his work and his people. Kouzes and Posner used the general's example to conclude that, "Leadership is not an affair of the head; it is an affair of the heart."

My grandfather, Homer O. Hewitt, was an executive on the Norfolk and Western Railway (presently, the Norfolk Southern Railway). Since my father was killed in the South Pacific in World War II, I was mostly raised by my grandparents. Mr. Hewitt was a Lucky Strike smoking, whiskey-drinking, hard-nosed labor negotiator who gave the unions fits. He wrote sixteen books on labor relations and worked 364½ days a year (he took Christmas morning off). He had a disdain for compromise and sought to optimize every issue. As noted previously, I share his disdain for compromise because of its kinship with the compromise of one's convictions.

I rarely saw my grandfather (unless I wanted to get up at 5:00 a.m. and listen to him explain his day to my grandmother over cigarettes and coffee), but on an occasional Saturday, he would take me to his big office in downtown Roanoke, Virginia and let me push the buttons under his desk that permitted him to "buzz for his assistants." Together with the work, the cigarettes, and the Lord Calvert whiskey, he died at fifty-five years of age. Although I am not a smoker or whiskey drinker, I share my grandfather's work ethic and his desire to document his knowledge so that others might benefit.

Henry Miller wrote that, "A man writes to throw off the poison, which he has accumulated because of his false way of life. He is trying to recapture his innocence." I am sure that I created some poison in my youth and in my failures as a leader. Time has taught me much and hopefully, my readers will find some wisdom herein and develop a brave heart to weather the storms of responsibility and the thorns of criticism that accompany the privilege of leadership. I have tried to share what I have learned from my experience, supported by the incidents that served as my classroom. I may have learned the wrong lessons and doubt all will agree with all my assertions. If I have accomplished my mission with this book, my readers will use the highlighter frequently. Leadership author, Max DePree, referred to it as "finishing" what you read. If you read this book without sensing the need to highlight or write in the margins, then I have failed to deliver any wisdom, insight, or anything memorable.

REFERENCES

The Holy Bible, New International Version

Allen, James. *As a Man Thinketh*

Aurelius, Marcos. *Meditations of Marcos Aurelius*

Bennis, Warren and Nanus, Burt, *Leaders: The Strategies for Taking Charge*

Benson, James, *So You Want to Be a Leader*

Brown, Steven, *13 Fatal Errors Managers Make and How You Can Avoid Them*

Bunting, Josiah, III. *An Education for Our Time*

Cambon, Jules. http://www:wikiwand.com/en/Jules_Cambon

Carnegie, Dale. *How to Develop Confidence and Influence People by Public Speaking*

Carnegie, Dale. *How to Win Friends and Influence People*

Carter, Stephen. *Integrity*

Charan, Ram. "It's Time to Split HR," *The Harvard Business Reivew*, July-August, 2014

Cleland, Max. *Heart of a Patriot*

Cloud, Henry. *Integrity: The Courage to Meet the Demands of* Reality

Cloud, Henry. *Necessary Endings*

Cockerell, Lee. *Creating Magic: 10 Common Sense Leadership Strategies from a Life At Disney*

Coleridge, Samuel. http://wikipedia.org/wiki/Samuel_Coleridge

Daniel, T. L. "Managerial Behavior: Their Relationship to Perceived Organizational Climate in a High-Technology Company." *Group and Organizational Studies*

Deming, W. Edwards. *Total Quality Management*

Depree, Max. *Leadership is an Art*

Dinger, J. E. http://www.quotes.net/authors/J.E.Dinger

Disraeli, Benjamin. http://www.quotationspage.com/quotes/Benjamin_Disraeli

Drucker, Peter. *The Effective Executive*

Euripides. http://www:goodreads.com/author/quotes/1973.Euripides

Franklin, Benjamin. *Benjamin Franklin, the Autobiography and Other Writings*

Franklin, Benjamin. *Poor Richard's Almanac*

Friedman, Edwin. *A Failure of Nerve*

Gaither, Jerry. *Hubbard's Law*

Gardner, John. *On Leadership*

Geneen, Harold. *Managing*

Goethe, Johann Wolfgang Von. https://www.bing.com/images/search ?q=johann+wolfgang+von+goethe

Hankey, Donald. *The Beloved Captain*

Hardy, Darren. *The Compound Effect*

Haas, Robert. "Values Made the Company," *Harvard Business Review*, September, 1990

Hayaski, A. M. *When to Trust Your God*

Heilman, E. B. *An Interruption That Lasted a Lifetime*

Henil, R. D., Jr. *Dictionary of Military and Naval Quotations*

Hilton, Conrad. *Be My Guest*

Holmes, Oliver. http://www.brainyquotes.com/oliver_wendall_holmes

Hubbard, Elbert. http://www.quotationspage.com/quotes/Elbert_ Hubbard

Jackson, Gerald. *Executive ESP*

Jones, John Paul. *"Inspirational Journeys," www.goodreads.com*

Josephson, Michael. http://www.goodreads.com/author/ quotes/1090178Michael_Josephson

Kanna, Tarun. "Contextual Intelligence." *Harvard Business Review*, September, 2014

Kanter, Rosabeth Moss. *Confidence*

Khayet, Robert. *The Education of a Lifetime*

Kipling, Rudyard. *Second Jungle Book*

Kirke, Edmund. *The Rear-Guard of the Revolution*

Knight, Bobby. *His Own Man*

Kouzes, James M. and Posner, Barry Z. *The Leadership Challenge*

Kriegel, Robert J. and Patler, Louis. *If it Ain't Broke … Break It*

Lawrence, George. *Great Men Bow Down*

Lutz, Robert. *Car Guys Versus Bean Counters*

Lutz, Robert. *Guts*

Lutz, Robert. *Icons and Idiots*

Lytle, Clyde, Editor. *Leaves of Gold*

Machiavelli, Niccolò. *The Prince*

Mackay, Harvey. *Beware the Naked Man Who Offers You His Shirt*

Mackay, Harvey. *Swim With the Sharks*

Mallory, John. https://en.wikipedia.org/wiki/John_Mallory

Manchester, William. http://www.brainyquote.com/quotes/authors/w/william_manchester.html

Mannes, Marya. http://brainyquotes.com/quotes/authors/M/Marya/Mannes

Marshall, S.L.A. http://en/wikiquotes.org/wiki/S.L.A._Marshall

Maxwell, John. *The Indispensable Qualities of a Leader*

McCormick, Mark. *What They Don't Teach You at the Harvard Business School*

Miller, Henry. http://www.brainyquotes.com/quotes/authors/h/henry_miller

Miller, Zell. *Corps Values*

Mintzberg, Henry and Quinn, James. *The Strategy Process*

Mohler, Albert. *The Conviction to Lead*

Moore, Hal. *A Tender Warrior*

Neeley, Tsedal and Leonardi, Paul. "Effective Managers Say the Same Thing Twice," *Harvard Business Review*, May, 2011

Newberry, Tommy and Beavers, Curt. *I Call Shotgun*

Novak, David. http://www.forbes.com/sites/kevinkruse/2014/06/25/david_novak_leadership

O'Brien, Michael. *Vince*

Owen, Harrison. *The Spirit of Leadership*

Paterno, Joe. *Paterno: By the Book*

Patton, George S. Jr. *War as I Knew It*

Peters, Tom and Austin, Nancy. *A Passion for Excellence*

Phillips, Donald T. *Lincoln on Leadership*

Pierce, Richard. *Leadership Perspective and Restructuring for Total Quality*

Pollard, William. *The Soul of the Firm*

Powell, Colin. *It Worked For Me: In Life and Leadership*

Rickover, Hyman. http://www.wikipedia.ord/wiki/Hyman_Rickover

Riley, Pat. *The Winner Within*

Ringer, Robert. *Million Dollar Habits*

Ringer, Robert. *The Natural Law of Balance*

Roberts, Wess. *Leadership Secrets of Attila the Hun*

Rockefeller, John D. http://www.brainyquotes.com/quotes/authors/John_D_Rockefeller

Rosemond, John. *Richmond Times-Dispatch*

Rutland, Mark. *Relaunch*

Seybert, Jim. *The One Year Mini for Leaders*

Shanahan, John, Editor. *The Most Brilliant Thoughts of All Time*

Shaw, George Bernard. http://www.biography.com/people/george_bernard_shaw

Staples, Walter D. *Think Like a Winner*

Steiglitz, Harold. "Chief Executives View Their Jobs: Today and Tomorrow." *The Conference Report*

Stockdale, James B. "Educating Leaders," *The Washington Quarterly*, July 13, 2009

Sun-Tsu. *The Art of War*

Tillich, Paul. https://en.wikipedia.org/wiki/Paul_Tillich

Townsend, Robert. *Up the Organization*

Trulock, Alice Rains. *In the Hands of Providence: Joshua L. Chamberlain and the American Civil War*

Waitley, Denis. *Empires of the Mind*

Walsh, Bill. *Building a Champion*

Walton, Mary. *The Deming Management Method*

West, Marvin. *Spizzerinctum-The Ray Bussard Story*

Zigler, Zig. *Life Promises for Leaders*

Zigler, Zig. *Over the Top*

"Discover to me, O my God, the nothingness of this world; the greatness of heaven, the shortness of time, and the length of eternity."

Universal Prayer of Clement XI

ABOUT THE AUTHOR

Jim Benson began his professional career as a high school teacher and football and baseball coach in Roanoke, Virginia. However, with the Vietnam war in the news, he felt the calling to lead in an environment where the stakes were higher, and there was less fame and recognition, so he signed up for Officer Candidates School, shipped off to Quantico, Virginia for what began a 26-year career as a Marine officer. By summer of 1969, he was an infantry platoon commander in Quang Nam Province, South Vietnam. Before the year was over, he became a company commander and went on the reach the rank of colonel before retiring in the summer of 1995.

At that time, he returned to his education background by serving as the Executive Assistant to the President and Director of Planning at Bridgewater College, soon moving up to the position of Vice President for Administration. In his book, *Executive Courage ...,* Jim describes this experience as an organizational *recovery* led by a dynamic president, Dr. Phillip C. Stone.

In 2004, he moved to Alabama where he became the 15th President of Marion Military Institute (MMI), a long-time struggling independent two-year college and high school college preparatory school. While at MMI, Jim was the author of the legislation that made the Institute a state-owned and funded military college, and culminated in a dramatic turnaround that solidified the college's future as the military college of the state of Alabama. Meanwhile, he filled over 200 empty beds, dramatically increased the revenue while reducing the expenses, and completed a major renovation of the campus and its facilities. He also kick-started a dismal fundraising program that raised over $8M in 5-years.

In 2009, Jim was recruited to rescue a failing Riverside Military Academy (RMA), a 102-year-old independent middle and secondary college preparatory school in Gainesville, GA. With superb facilities and a supportive Board of Trustees, the Academy was failing in virtually every operational area leaving the Board with the question of whether to sell the school or try once more to turn it around. Losing millions of dollars annually with over 200 empty beds, bloated expenditures, no fundraising program to speak of, unhappy alumni and more, Jim began a seven-year turnaround that filled virtually every bed, significantly reduced expenses, and raised the annual revenues from less than $10M to just short of $20M.

Jim resigned the presidency of RMA in the summer of 2016 and immediately began his consulting career. Since then he has served as Principal Officer for J.H. Benson Turnarounds and Recoveries, LLC, and has worked to improve the financial/business practices, personnel management, educational and residential life programs, athletic programs, enrollment management systems, and fundraising programs of independent educational institutions. Additionally, he has worked with governing boards relative to management team selection and hiring as well as other forms of counsel. Lastly, Jim works with non-educational businesses to develop their Long Range/Strategic Plans, assist with executive searches, analyze and recommend changes to their organizational structure, examine and recommend relative to business and financial practices, and write or rewrite their foundational documents. Jim presently serves as Chairman of the Board of Directors at Atlanta Paving and Concrete Construction, Inc.

Jim's military career included assignments as Commanding Officer Joint Task Force 129, Special Operations and Counter-Terrorism; Commanding Officer, 6th Marine Regiment; and Chief of Staff/Assistant Commander of the 2nd Marine Division. A decorated veteran, Jim was awarded the Defense Superior Service Medal, three Legion of Merit Awards, two Bronze Star Medals with "V" for Valor, the Meritorious Service Medal, the Joint Service Commendation Medal, the Vietnamese Cross of Gallantry with Palm, three Navy Commendation Medals one with "V" for Valor, and the Navy Achievement Medal.

Jim's first book, *So You Want to Be a Leader? Advice and Counsel to Young Leaders* was published by Trafford Publishing Company in 2007. The second edition was published in 2013.

Jim received a Bachelor of Arts degree from Bridgewater College, a Master of Science degree from the University of Tennessee, a Master of Public Administration degree from the Pennsylvania State University and a Doctorate of Higher Education Administration from The George Washington University. He is also a graduate of the Armed Forces Staff College and the Army War College.

Jim can be contacted at jhbenson15@gmail.com or (678)622-3604.

NOTES